CITY of ANGELS

CITY OF ANGELS
Houses and Gardens of Los Angeles

PHOTOGRAPHY BY
Firooz Zahedi

TEXT BY
Jennifer Ash Rudick

VENDOME
NEW YORK · LONDON

CONTENTS

INTRODUCTION 7

EUROPEAN INTRIGUE 13

BEVERLY HILLS ARCADIA 35

GLOBAL VIEW 51

CRISP ELEGANCE IN
HOLLYWOOD HILLS 61

BEL AIR COSMOPOLITAN 79

INTERNATIONAL HIGH STYLE 93

ARGYLE FARM 105

EDWARDS HOUSE 123

BUNGALOWS 135

Artist's Palette 135

Passion Play 145

California Bountiful 154

Urban Zen 159

Perfectly Imperfect 163

Neutra Revisited 170

SIMPLICITY AND SPACE 179

ART DECO OPULENCE 191

RAW AND REFINED 209

LYRICAL BEAUTY 227

GARCIA HOUSE 247

INDEPENDENT THINKING 261

CLASSICISM IN HANCOCK
PARK 279

SEASIDE CLARITY 297

ELEMENTS OF STYLE 313

MODERNISM REDEFINED 331

GEORGIAN REDUX 345

VISUAL JOURNEY 361

CALIFORNIA DREAMING 377

ACKNOWLEDGMENTS 390

INTRODUCTION

IN SETTING, SIZE, EXTERIOR DESIGN, AND interior décor, houses are often seen as the visual manifestation of their inhabitants' personality, lifestyle, and aesthetic. And perhaps nowhere is this link between biography and residence of greater fascination than in Los Angeles, where an entire ecosystem of bus tours and star maps has evolved to give legions of avid fans a sense of connection to the lives of their favorite celebrities by catching a glimpse of their homes.

I first visited Los Angeles at age ten in the mid-1970s. Our vacation promised hiking and horseback riding in Beverly Glen—plans that were abruptly redirected when I stumbled barefoot onto the smoldering coals of a barbecue pit in the Hollywood Hills. My family and I spent the rest of the week in a leased convertible exploring neighborhoods threaded together by ribbons of highways, an urban sprawl not unfamiliar to a Florida native. I saw mid-century glass cubes perched dramatically on hillsides, Mediterranean-style mansions shielded behind curtains of palms, charming bungalows, and smart, stylish Regencies. We breezed in and out of the Los Angeles County Museum of Art and the Getty Villa; hardly art world heavyweights back then, they didn't attract the crowds that they do now. Recently, L.A.'s design scene has burst into prominence like an endless fireworks display, catapulting its artists, architects, and interior decorators to renown on the world stage.

No chronicle of L.A. interiors would be complete without featuring the residences of some of the city's growing wave of enterprising and community-minded art dealers, artists, and patrons, including Margo Leavin, Sarah Gavlak, Jane and Marc Nathanson, Don Bachardy, Mandy and Cliff Einstein, Steve Tisch, and Darren Star. Beth Rudin DeWoody and Firooz Zahedi's vertical compound perfectly reflects their shared vision of collecting. Zahedi's dazzling photographs on these pages not only capture the ineffable alchemy of good design but also personalize each residence, every image as soulful and revealing as the celebrity portraits for which he is famous.

Opposite • Beth Rudin DeWoody and Firooz Zahedi furnished the terrace of one of their three apartments in a building designed by modernist architect Victor Gruen with vintage mid-century modern furniture found in West Palm Beach. The flowers are from Empty Vase Florist in West Hollywood.

Above • A row of perfectly spaced and meticulously pruned trees lends a sublime sense of order to Susan Nimoy's airy Bel Air home.

A painting by California artist Gary Lang adds a jolt of color in the neutral-toned living room of Tony and Dierdre Graham's inviting mid-century modern house, designed by architect Rex Lotery, with an addition by architect Tim Campbell. Prudence, the Grahams' American cocker spaniel, is in perfect sync with the room's palette.

Though L.A. no longer revolves solely around the film industry, its character traits are forever sequenced in the city's DNA. The entertainment world is all about individual style, and what greater signifier of one's creative chops is there than how one lives? L.A. interior designers have always understood that a personal narrative is as crucial as decorative refinement. Their unique brand of casual sophistication has been translated around the world, perhaps most prominently in the work of Michael S. Smith, who was commissioned to decorate the private quarters of the Obama White House. Kelly Wearstler, Madeline Stuart, Suzanne Rheinstein, Hutton Wilkinson, Oliver Furth, Mark D. Sikes, Cliff Fong, David Netto, and mid-century house sorcerer Mark Haddawy all enjoy national acclaim.

Mid-century modern continues to be an iconic style in Los Angeles, just as Anglo-Indian is in the Caribbean, Mediterranean Revival in Palm Beach, and Shingle Style on the East Coast. Mid-century houses by John Lautner, Richard Neutra, Harold Levitt, Edward H. Fickett, Rex Lotery, and Victor Gruen, all featured on these pages, are experiencing a second life in the hands of L.A.'s working architects. Rather than flex her own aesthetic muscles, "starchitect" Pamela Shamshiri restored a residence by Viennese modernist Rudolph Schindler for herself and her family. A Buff, Straub & Hensman design, partially drafted by California's leading architectural light, Frank Gehry, when he was a USC student, is home to Cynthia Wornham and Ann Philbin, director of the Hammer Museum, which is increasing its gallery size by 70 percent; the new galleries will be designed in turn by Michael Maltzan, a Gehry student.

The following pages also present the best of L.A.'s Regencies, Georgians, Mediterraneans, and bungalows. Despite their disparate styles, all of the houses share the organic coherence and lived-in authenticity that accrue only over time and not just when propped for a photo shoot.

In her late eighties, my mother moved cross-country to California—one way to navigate old age with grace. When I asked her why she had waited so long to head west, she answered, "Darling, I got here as fast as I could!" An indisputable argument for why *now* is always the moment to heed the call of the new. Although our homes ultimately tell the story of our lives, it's never too late to change—or should I say edit, or rethink—the narrative.

Below • In the living room of a neo-Georgian house with interiors designed by Oliver Furth, a Morris Louis painting finds a common language with an antique récamier sofa.

Overleaf • An Alexander Calder stabile presides over the pool in Jane and Marc Nathanson's clean, contemporary garden.

EUROPEAN INTRIGUE

A TRANSCENDENT HOLMBY HILLS compound serves as a veritable lab for the evolving taste of furniture designer, sculptor, and inveterate collector Richard Shapiro. A former trustee of Los Angeles's Museum of Contemporary Art, Shapiro's reimagining of a Hispano-Moorish house, built in the 1920s, pays homage to the great European estates he visited on museum-led trips. "Being an art collector was an entrée to visit a lot of homes, which was an epiphany. I studied the architecture and interiors as closely as I did the art." Shapiro's observations honed his irrepressible instinct to shape the world around him, and his house reflects the design ideas that he has been amassing and refining for more than thirty years. "The more you see and study, the better your intuition."

Following a successful career in the car-rental business, Shapiro first indulged his creative hankering with the opening of the Beverly Hills steakhouse The Grill on the Alley in 1984. Its leather booths, brass lanterns, and artfully hung assortment of framed drawings evoked an English men's club and became an instant hotspot.

Two years later, he purchased his Holmby Hills house and immediately set about "Europeanizing" it. Where an ordinary lawn and walkway had connected the front door to the sidewalk, Shapiro created a gravel motor court dramatically walled by what has grown into a forty-foot-high ficus hedge. "I wanted to create a sense of mystery."

To the casual observer, interiors of gouged-wood floors, faux finishes, and countless decorative objects and works of art might seem arbitrary, but they are in fact artfully articulated layers from varying periods and provenances. A Tatsuo Miyajima LED *Counter* sculpture and 192 pieces from Allan McCollum's *Surrogate* series mix with a late Roman bust and a gilt-wood console. "It's not precious. It's about good intellectual pieces and how they dialogue with other pieces around them. It's about self-deception, about feeling you could be anywhere, anytime."

A visit to the gardens of Villa Chiericati in Italy's Veneto region brought about the transformation of a grass lawn into an acre of topiaries. Shapiro imported more than 3,000 boxwood shrubs from a grower in Oregon,

Opposite • A circular painting by California artist Gary Lang is in striking contrast to the original 1920s banister. On the landing, petrified dinosaur eggs rest on a seventeenth-century Italian cabinet.

Above • A twentieth-century wood maquette of a staircase adorns the dining room.

outlined the placement of their groupings with chalk, and had them clipped into abstract shapes. Sinuously curving gravel walkways meander through this topiary garden. He camouflaged the nearby pool with algae-green paint and distressed-stone coping.

Just as English aristocrats of the eighteenth century constructed neoclassical follies as shelters in their gardens, Shapiro commissioned a poolside re-creation of a sixteenth-century Palladian portico, complete with twenty-one-foot-high columns. And he engaged a set designer to age the columns with a mixture of plaster, lime, and spray-painted moss.

Shapiro's own monumental, abstract steel sculptures dot the property. "I started producing art in the mid-'90s. I just had the urge." Eventually he added an enormous glass-walled studio to the property. "There's scarcely a square foot that I haven't modified," admits Shapiro. "In all honesty, I wanted to deceive myself. I wanted to pretend I was in Italy. Even to this day. All these years later, I still appreciate being transported."

Opposite • Boston ivy covers the façade of the 1920s Hispano-Moorish house. The door is original.

Below left • Shapiro fashioned the bases of twin tables from the roots of a large Japanese tree and topped them with slate. A 1953 work by Shozo Shimamoto, a co-founder of the Japanese Gutai group, hangs over the sofa.

Below right • A collection of sculpted heads ranging from the Hellenistic period through the nineteenth century decorates a tabletop. A Moroccan damascened urn was found in Marrakech.

Overleaf • In the living room, Ewerdt Hilgemann's stainless-steel *Implosion* hangs over the fireplace. The Minima sofa and pair of chairs are from the Richard Shapiro Studiolo Collection.

Pages 18–19 • The cavernous dining room doubles as a gallery. To the left of the mantel is an LED *Counter* sculpture by Tatsuo Miyajima. On the floor to the right is a Carl Andre *Timber* sculpture. 192 pieces from Allan McCollum's *Surrogates* series hangs on the right. A 1940s French table is surrounded by nineteenth-century Regency-style chairs covered in a blue-and-white gingham.

Left • A Piero Fornasetti secretary, 1950, is flanked by a bronze-and-steel sculpture by Anthony Caro and a Hans Wegner Flag Halyard chair.

Below • An early eighteenth-century armchair interacts with a Plaine de Couleurs table from the Richard Shapiro Studiolo Collection. The painting over the cabinet is an unattributed seventeenth-century Italian work; the c-print over the sofa is Jean-Pierre Khazem's *Mona Lisa Live*.

Opposite • Among the artworks in the library are two Rudolf Stingel paintings and a vintage photograph of Egypt. The rug is Moroccan and was found in Fez.

Overleaf • Shapiro commissioned a large Florian Baudrexel cardboard sculpture, 2015, for the upstairs landing. Hanging to its left is one of his own paintings.

Above left • In the addition, a Jacques Lipchitz gouache rests on an eighteenth-century bench next to an English lay figure seated on a primitive three-legged chair.

Above right • The many books and the globe reveal Shapiro's penchant for reading, research, and travel.

Left • A combination of Fior di Pesco, white Carrara, and Negro Marquina marbles adorns the master bath.

Opposite • Shapiro found the bed canopy while traveling in Jaipur. The console is eighteenth-century French.

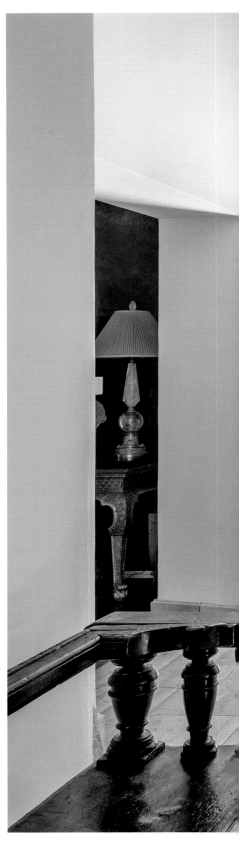

Over the console are a soot painting by Otto Piene and a fourth-century A.D. Roman marble head. A latex rubber cast relief of a window by California artist Robert Overby hangs above the small cabinet.

A bronze sculpture by Tony Smith anchors the "galleria."

Above • Shapiro created this three-dimensional, welded-steel sculpture of a Brice Marden drawing.

Opposite • Shapiro studied the plans and dimensions in Palladio's *I Quattro Libri dell'Architettura* to build an exact replica of the portico at Villa Chiericati.

Opposite and this page • Inspired by the gardens of Villa Chiericati, Shapiro transformed a grass lawn into an acre of boxwood topiaries.

Overleaf left • Modern urns line a walkway to a nineteenth-century French fountain found in Nice.

Overleaf right, clockwise from top left • An eighteenth-century French millstone; a wood and plaster sculpture by Shapiro, inspired by the Dutch De Stijl movement; a timber piece, also by Shapiro, inspired by Hans Arp; an eighteenth-century Italian bust.

BEVERLY HILLS
ARCADIA

DIERDRE AND TONY GRAHAM'S DREAM of moving into an arresting mid-century modern house originally designed by Rex Lotery appeared to be dashed when they lost it to another buyer. "My husband wasn't ready to move and it sold while we went back and forth, but we couldn't get it off our minds," says Dierdre. So when the house went back on the market two years later, they pounced. The stylish glass cube, set on a large, cloistered property along one of Beverly Hills' most central and desirable streets, is the kind of place that leaves an indelible impression.

The Grahams set about to restore, but not enshrine, the 1960 house, which was conceived when kitchens and bathrooms were small and closets were not designed with a couple who are considered cornerstones of L.A.'s fashion business in mind. Enter award-winning architect Tim Campbell. "The only way to save these historic houses is to make them relevant. Someone from the Getty told me, 'When I restore a painting, you should not know I was there at all.' That's my goal. I want to improve the structure but I don't want to leave my mark," says Campbell, who performed a surgical intervention on the existing structure and also conceived an addition that would provide a study, a guest room, and a larger kitchen for the family of four. Campbell designed the addition with his typical restraint, setting it a few feet back from the original structure. "The new pavilion sits a little less proud but mindful. I like to think of additions as backup singers," supporting but not overshadowing the original design. He drew inspiration from the huge expanses of glass and the pavilion-style roof, with its deep overhang. "Rex Lotery houses are sexy. The original pavilion with the terrace that extends from it is called the adult playroom. It's very open and designed to show off the fact that people are having a fantastic life. With this design, Lotery wasn't shy, rather, almost voyeuristic." In both the original structure and the addition, enormous windows emphasize indoor-outdoor fluidity; bright rooms merge with shaded terraces, giving way to sleek gardens, the unmistakable work of landscape designer Art Luna.

Opposite and above • Dierdre and Tony Graham's mid-century modern house, originally designed in 1960 by Rex Lottery, emphasizes indoor-outdoor fluidity. The gardens were designed by Art Luna, who sculpted a sloping front lawn into stadium seating bordered by *Pittosporum tobira* hedges.

Top and bottom right •
Honed bluestone pavers lead
past a water feature, original
to Lotery's design, to the
front door. Grasses soften
the façade.

Lauded for his hybrid style of free-flowing yet formal gardens, Luna famously honed his craft by shearing Hollywood's most beautiful heads. Clients so admired the garden he created for his salon that they began begging him to design for them. "I always try to bring out the soul of the garden, just like you always try to reflect the soul of a person when you work on their hair," says Luna. The Grahams' garden incorporates resting areas for reflection and unexpected elements such as crystals. Behind the house, winding, stepped paths lead to the top of a hill where an Airstream—installed using a crane—serves as a retreat.

The couple called upon Poonam Khanna to conceive the interior finishes, fixtures, and millwork. She set the tone by using the back sides of bronze slabs for the entrance hall fireplace surround. "I knew Tony and Dierdre would appreciate the rawness of it," says Khanna.

For the décor, the couple turned to an old friend from the fashion business, former buyer, merchandiser, and master of nuance Cliff Fong, who was thriving in his second act as an interior designer. "Tony and Dierdre have great style from top to bottom, and they don't dress or live to impress. They're more about high/low and the unexpected, and they're also very warm, casual, and unfussy. I wanted the house to reflect who they are." To that end, he incorporated vintage ethnic fabrics and African elements, drawing on Tony's heritage. "A few pieces of furniture really brought the house together," including an architectural leather chair from Arne Jacobsen. "It's an example of something that could be precious but treated in a casual way—that's the Grahams."

Award-winning architect Tim Campbell was charged with restoring Rex Lotery's design. In the entrance hall, the sofa and chair are by Tobia Scarpa, the floor lamp is from Vintage Art, and the sculpture is from JF Chen.

Opposite top • In the lower living room of the original structure, or "adult playroom," as Rex Lotery called it, is an Ox chair by Hans Wegner. The coffee table is by Brian Thoreen and the rug is by Amadi Carpets. A painting by Gary Lang adds a pop of color.

Opposite bottom • In the entrance hall, a Rodney Graham *Inverted Drip Painting* and a Serge Mouille four-arm sconce hang over a Charlotte Perriand cabinet.

Right • Kilim runners from Woven warm up the hallway.

Below • In the library, a Hans Wegner Flag Halyard chair sits next to a small wood side table by Michael Wilson, found at JF Chen. The 1930 Axel Einar Hjorth Uto coffee table was found at Galerie Half.

Overleaf • An Amadi rug lies in front of a built-in sofa covered in cream custom linen. The tripartite anthracite coffee table is by Jim Zivic. An Arne Jacobsen Oksen lounge chair sits in one corner.

Left • A modern sectional Tufty-Time sofa, designed by Patricia Urquiola for B&B Italia, blends with a George Nakashima live-edge coffee table, ca. 1971, found at Galerie Half. The hanging sculpture, *Vintage Pawn Balls*, is from de Vera in New York.

Below • A Hugh Scott-Douglas blue cyanotype print on linen hangs to the right, and Al Taylor's *Helen*, 1976, to the left.

Opposite top • In the dining room, a Rick Owens chandelier hangs over a BDDW table surrounded by vintage Paul Evans sculpted-bronze dining chairs. A narrow mosaic by Joe Conforti runs along two walls.

Opposite bottom • In the kitchen, vintage stools are upholstered in mohair.

Opposite top left • In the master bath, the sheepskin-covered stool is by Paul McCobb.

Opposite top right • A vintage desk and chair by Pierre Jeanneret take center stage in a guest bedroom.

Opposite bottom • The master bedroom is furnished with a pair of nightstands and a sideboard by George Nakashima. The vintage lamps on the nightstands are by Swedish lighting designer Hans-Agne Jakobsson.

Above • In the guest bedroom, a pair of lounge chairs with adjustable backs and leather seats by Kai Lyngfeldt Larsen, found at JF Chen, flank a low, organically shaped wood coffee table by Michael Wilson. Vintage iron, leather, and brass nightstands were found at Hollywood at Home. The lithograph is by Louise Nevelson.

Left • Six concrete chairs by Willy Guhl blend into the landscape and create an intimate seating area.

Below • Large bronze pots on the upper terrace are planted with citrus trees.

Opposite, clockwise from top left • Creeping fig climbs a wall; a long series of wooden steps ascends the steep back yard; Art Luna often incorporates crystals such as these from Belo Horizonte in Malibu into his garden designs to generate positive energy; star jasmine covers a wall in an area of the garden furnished with stone chairs that Tony Graham found in South Africa.

Overleaf • A vintage Airstream was installed by crane in the upper reaches of the property next to an outdoor seating area, creating an enticing retreat.

GLOBAL VIEW

OVER THE PAST FORTY YEARS, JOEL CHEN has evolved from a go-to source for Asian rarities into the city's international design curator in chief. An encyclopedic knowledge of decorative arts and a profound intuition for what's next fuels the continued success of his multicultural treasure trove called JF Chen—a 40,000-square-foot, warehouse-size gallery in Los Angeles's Highland Avenue and Santa Monica Boulevard neighborhood. Chen is tickled, if a little bemused, by his stature as an elder statesman of L.A.'s latest design explosion. His client list reads like a Who's Who at the intersection of the city's entertainment, design, and art worlds, ranging from Harry Styles and Adele to Tracy Chapman, Barbra Streisand, and Sean Parker. Both Peter Marino and Michael Smith make pilgrimages, as do Alexander Wang, Bruce Weber, Christian Louboutin, and those unlikely arbiters of good taste, the Olsen twins.

Chen's own house, which he shares with his wife, Margaret, is an English Tudor affair in historic Hancock Park, which he found "long before all of the strollers arrived." The interiors are equally prescient, reflecting the adventurous sensibility of a curator who has spent his professional life ahead of the curve, traveling beyond the usual interior-designer trades routes of England, France, and Italy. Chen sourced painted furniture in Slovenia, Czechoslovakia, and Hungary. He bought Art Deco in Turkey, discovered Anglo-Indian furniture in Goa and French antiques in Argentina, and imported mid-century modern designs from Denmark.

Vignettes scattered around his house reflect his global view. "There are so many beautiful things in the world and so many ways to put them together, I just can't make up my mind." The entrance hall alone mixes a French Carrara marble bust, a nineteenth-century mirrored exclamation mark—a gift from the artist Rob Wynne—a nineteenth-century Continental mixed-metal sculpture of a turkey, an Anglo-Indian box, and a second-century A.D. marble torso from the MGM estate. The great room includes a neoclassical bronze inkwell, a Chinese Ming/Song dynasty gold-and-bronze censer in the shape of a mystical bird, and an eighteenth-century Italian gilt-wood painted column from Hearst Castle.

Opposite • In the entrance hall, a glass exclamation mark, a gift from the artist Rob Wynne, hangs over an eighteenth-century gilt-wood Italian pedestal topped by a French Carrara marble bust of Diana. In the dining room beyond, the chairs are by Saridis, and the curtains are a Manuel Canovas fabric.

Above • Vases by Georges Jouve sit atop an eighteenth-century Italian gilt-wood pedestal table.

Many of the pieces were bought specifically for the house, but some were retrieved from his shop. "Everything of mine has a chance to sell until it doesn't. And if it starts to grow on me, then I put it in my house. I have an enormous collection already, so whatever I add needs to speak to me a lot. But once it's in the house, it stays. Nothing here is for sale."

The internet has diminished Chen's need to travel, but the hunt, if virtual, still thrills him. He hankers for "a Prouvé atelier or tropical house," he says, referring to a 1949 prototype of an inexpensive, readily assembled house that French metalworker, architect, and furniture designer Jean Prouvé conceived for France's African colonies. "The idea of someone being able to live with 5 pieces in a 2,000-square-foot house? I tip my hat to them. I couldn't do it."

Opposite • The stenciled floors in the entrance hall and throughout the house were inspired by the work of designer Thomas Britt.

Above left • Statues of the Baby Jesus from Peru, Spain, Italy, and France sit on top of a commode by Syrie Maugham. A limited-edition Maarten Baas red chair was found at Art Basel. The two small paintings are nineteenth-century French beach scenes.

Above right • A George Nakashima coffee table anchors the living room. The painting is by Charles Safford and the side chair is by mid-century architect and designer Carlo Mollino.

Overleaf • The large vase on the pedestal in the living room is by Danish ceramicist Per Weiss. The cabinets flanking it were designed by Ole Wanscher. The vessel on the three-legged table in front of the fireplace is by Tove Anderberg. A Neo-Dadaist sculpture on the far right of the fireplace mantel is by Soroku Toyoshima.

Preceding pages • In the dining room, a Biedermeier cabinet sits under an Op Art work by D. Nolanz, ca. 1966. A green lacquered-parchment mirror from the 1970s hangs over an eighteenth-century English console.

Above • A nineteenth-century Japanese silver-leaf screen dominates a section of wall in a large room. The sofa is in the style of Jean-Michel Frank. Atop a pedestal is an eighteenth-century painted Italian Nubian statue. The table is laden with Chen's collection of design books.

Left • A chair by Krueck and Sexton is covered in teal velvet. The eighteenth-century pillars were originally in Hearst Castle.

A nineteenth-century Japanese screen hangs between chairs upholstered in the style of Billy Baldwin. A round Anglo-Indian table centers the room.

CRISP ELEGANCE
IN HOLLYWOOD HILLS

WHEN MARK D. SIKES AND HIS PARTNER, Michael Griffin, relocated to Los Angeles, he craved a traditional, two-story house with a central hall, a perfect backdrop for everything he loves: simple elegance derived from textural neutrals and a combination of rustic and glamorous pieces, much in the vein of the narrative he communicated as a former visual merchandiser for Pottery Barn and Banana Republic. "Linen curtains blowing in the wind, chinoiserie mixed with wicker, natural-fiber rugs, English rolled-arm sofas, gilt consoles mixed with modern art, that sort of thing."

After finding a house in the Hollywood Hills that was "convenient to everything," Sikes infused the interiors with air and light, whitewashing floors and painting walls in a soft linen color. Wanting to blur the lines between indoors and out, he turned his attention to the garden, which was a vertiginous tangle of weeds. "When we got in and started digging and terracing, we carted out twelve truckloads of dirt. We were quite surprised at how big the garden really was. Suddenly we had a thousand square feet of additional living space."

The truckloads of dirt caught the attention of Sikes's neighbor, a scouting editor for *House Beautiful* magazine. The interiors and the now lush, terraced garden landed on the cover of the December 2011/January 2012 issue of *House Beautiful*, fast-tracking Sikes's interior design career. "Visual merchandising is not very different from designing a living room," Sikes says. "They are both creative endeavors whose implementation has deadlines and requires extreme organization, resourcefulness, and diplomacy," all of which Mark D. Sikes has in spades.

Opposite • In his Hollywood Hills house, Mark D. Sikes combines rustic and glamorous pieces to elegant effect. The banquette in the living room is upholstered in Archaism from Robert Allen.

Above • A tabletop vignette in the living room includes a bust found on a European trip and a blue-and-white ceramic planter from JF Chen.

Above, opposite, and overleaf • The dining room (opposite) and living room (overleaf) lie on either side of the entrance hall (above). Sikes infused the interiors with air and light, whitewashing floors and painting walls in a soft linen color. In the dining room, he used Brunschwig & Fils' Les Touches for the curtains and covered the chairs in Moore & Giles's Doral leather. In the living room, the club chairs are upholstered in Quadrille's Veneto. A Billy Baldwin slipper chair can be pulled up for supplementary seating.

Preceding pages • Carolina Irving's Patmos Stripe swaths a guest bedroom that also houses Sikes's collection of shelter and fashion magazines.

Left • Pendant fixtures from Visual Comfort hang above Carrara marble counters in the kitchen.

Below • An inviting, book-lined seating area in the kitchen features a sofa covered in a Jasper fabric and a George Smith tufted-leather ottoman.

Opposite • A handsome iron banister, bird prints, and a mirror bring buoyancy to the sky-lit staircase.

Opposite left, top right, and center right • In a guest bedroom, Pierre Frey's Le Grand Genois Rayure is used for the bed hangings, walls, chair, and ottoman.

Opposite bottom right • In a nearby powder room, a Regency ebony-and-bone mirror hangs above a Gramercy Single Metal sink from Restoration Hardware. The beadboard and trim are painted Benjamin Moore's high-gloss black.

Right and below • A Gracie hand-painted wallpaper creates an ethereal atmosphere in the master bedroom. The small sofa at the foot of the bed is covered in Raoul Textiles' Patra.

Opposite and above • The table overlooking the garden is set with pieces from services by Tory Burch and Bunny Williams, punctuated by items collected over the years.

Overleaf • Sikes turned the garden, which was a tangle of weeds when he moved in, into a terraced, manicured, thousand-square-foot extension of the house.

Above and opposite • Creeping fig is fast covering the house. An antique stone table comes from Inner Gardens, and the seating is from Restoration Hardware's Catalina Collection. Nothing says Hollywood chic like a black-and-white awning.

BEL AIR
COSMOPOLITAN

REDESIGNING A 1930S BEL AIR HOUSE

on a gentrified street off of Wilshire Boulevard proved a satisfying extension of Darren Star's creative process, a course of action analogous to creating television's smash hits *Melrose Place* and *Sex and the City*. He spotted a brilliant subject, the muse spoke, the best in the business were assembled, and magic occurred. "I wasn't planning on moving, but when I walked into this house, my heart skipped a beat. I loved the old-school Hollywood vibe, the dramatic round room, the fireplace, the spectacular views—it was all there."

Originally designed by John Byers with his signature Mexican and Spanish flourishes, the house was updated with slender, modernist columns and Art Deco touches in the 1960s by architect James Dolena. The resulting combination is a uniquely California style referred to as Spanish Regency.

Star lived in the house for three years before calling upon longtime friend and architect Mark Rios to renovate the interiors and unlock the site's potential. "The goal of the renovation was to make the place cleaner and to unify its design language, but I realized there were incredible views on the side of the house that was then the garage and a warren of rooms, so we rethought the program." Rios converted the garage into a double-height family room that takes full advantage of the stunning panoramic view of Hollywood.

Star hankered for interiors that would serve as a quiet backdrop for his swelling art collection. "I tend to like a neutral environment with a Zen, peaceful vibe, and it works well with art." As it turns out, simple interiors require dexterity, so enter interior designer Waldo Fernandez, a master at melding delicacy and drama. "Waldo immediately understood the goals," Star says. Wooden doors and windows were replaced with iron versions, the library paneling was lacquered a rich chocolate. Overstuffed seating by Jean Royère, Émile-Jacques Ruhlmann, and Eugène Printz in creamy shades made the house feel at once inviting and stylish. The juxtaposition of muted glamour with edgy works by California artists, including John Baldessari, Ed Ruscha, Robert Therrien, Mike Kelley, John McLaughlin,

Opposite • A painting of a disco ball by Dave Muller and a portrait by Kehinde Wiley grace the entrance hall of television producer Darren Star's Bel Air house.

Above • *Sex and the City*, one of the TV series that Darren Star created, won seven Emmy Awards, including the 2000 award for Outstanding Comedy Series, which is discreetly displayed on a bookshelf in the family room.

Above and opposite •
The house was originally
designed in the late 1930s
in a Mediterranean style
by John Byers. In the 1960s
architect James Dolena added
modernist touches, including
the slender columns at the
entrance; the result was a
uniquely California style
known as Spanish Regency.
More recently, Tony Rios
renovated the interiors,
including such flourishes
as a floating staircase. At
the end of the entrance
hall, a sculpture by Thomas
Houseago sits on a pedestal.

Walead Beshty, and Mark Grotjahn, creates a frisson and an overall effect of grandeur void of ostentation.

The addition of a pool house and screening room has turned the property into a sort of compound. "I show everything from first-run movies to *What's Up, Doc?* It's nice to expose my young writing staff to the classics." Star hosts pool parties but swears that the events do not include bed hopping or backstabbing, as they do in his sizzling shows. Though his commute to work is a short, inspiring drive down Sunset Boulevard, "I have to tear myself away," he admits. Not unlike the feeling one gets when binging on a season of *Sex and the City*.

Overleaf • In the library, a semicircular sofa covered in a Holly Hunt fabric is flanked by a pair of vintage director's chairs by Luigi Caccia Dominioni.

Top left • A Candida Höfer photograph has pride of place in a seating area of the living room.

Bottom left • A painting by John McLaughlin hangs over the mantel.

Above • Works by Robert Therrien (left) and Mark Grotjahn hang over a Yamaha piano.

Overleaf • Among the furnishings in front of the bronze-clad fireplace in the family room are a pair of vintage Gianfranco Frattini lounge chairs and a pair of Eugène Printz small palmwood stools, ca. 1925. The leather-covered cocktail table is by Nicholas Mongiardo.

Above • In the dining room,
the table, chairs, and
sideboard are by Paul Evans.
The chandelier is vintage
Venini. The art, from left
to right, is by Gilbert and
George, Mike Kelley, and
Walead Beshty.

Opposite top • Rios converted
the garage into a double-
height family room that has a
sweeping view of Hollywood.

Opposite bottom •
The cabinetry in the kitchen
is by Bulthaup, and the
fittings are by Dornbracht.

Overleaf • The sun-drenched
back of the house offers
panoramic views.

INTERNATIONAL HIGH STYLE

CONJURING UP BUILDINGS THAT INSPIRE optimism and elevate society comes naturally to Bangkok-born, Japanese-trained, Los Angeles–based architect Kulapat Yantrasast. An associate of Pritzker Prize–winning Japanese architect Tadao Ando from 1996 to 2003, he worked on Ando's Sterling and Francine Clark Art Institute in Williamstown, Massachusetts, and Modern Art Museum of Fort Worth, Texas. He founded his own firm, wHY, in 2003, and his first commission was the Grand Rapids Art Museum in Michigan, completed in 2007. More recently, wHY transformed Wilshire Boulevard's abandoned Scottish Rite Masonic Temple into a private modern art museum. Still, creating his own home, from the ground up, proved daunting. "The process of designing my own house, though overwhelming, was enriching and profound. There are thousands of decisions to make, from grand to granular. Being aware and thoughtful about each of these decisions is life changing," says Yantrasast.

It all started with a postage stamp–sized lot in Venice, whose laid-back vibe and proximity to the beach gave Yantrasast the license to imagine the casual house of his dreams. An abbreviated wish list, including graciously proportioned rooms, a pool, and indoor-outdoor fluidity—a hallmark of the architect's design philosophy—challenged Venice's famously small lots. Things fell into place when Yantrasast envisioned a vertical arrangement with the pool on the main level, where its deck could serve as open-air connector to all the main rooms, a plan reminiscent of the traditional Thai houses of his childhood. "I spend most of my time in this main living space; I love being there so much from morning to night. The light changes and interacts with the concrete walls, the water, and the plants—it's truly my happy place."

Though the structure, composed of concrete, glass, and steel, strikes a minimalist note, the interiors are chock full of playful objects and furniture, reflecting Yantrasast's innate whimsy and creativity. "I really see the house as my living laboratory." Some pieces were created in collaboration with Bob Dornberger, the director of wHY Objects Workshop, while others are by Yantrasast's design heroes.

Opposite and above • Architect Kulapat Yantrasast designed his house in Venice vertically to maximize its tiny footprint. He positioned the pool on the main level; its deck serves as an open-air connector to all the public rooms.

Below • The line between art and furniture blurs in Yantrasast's living room. On the far left is a Frank Gehry cardboard Wiggle Side Chair, manufactured by Vitra. Next to it is an iconic La Chaise by Charles and Ray Eames. A Philip Arctander Clam Chair is paired with a Haas Brothers Hex Stool.

There's a Frank Gehry corrugated-cardboard chair, a pair of silver inflated-steel side chairs by the Polish designer Oskar Zięta, and a honeycombed-paper armchair by Tokujin Yoshioka. Thrown in for good measure are castaway items, including Turkish antique rug-making tools and a mechanic's tool cart that serves as a bar.

"My house is an oasis for global nomads, like me. A place where everything happens naturally."

Opposite, clockwise from top left • Yantrasast and Bob Dornberger, director of wHY's Objects Workshop, collaborated on the living room shelves; a 1950s pickle was bought at auction and the hamburger is by Sarah Bay Williams; wHY's Terroir Stool is made with rocks collected from the Los Angeles River; a tool cart, found at a Long Beach flea market, makes a perfect bar.

Overleaf • The interior of the austere concrete, glass, and steel house is brimming with playful objects and furniture. The sofa is from wHY Objects. The table in the foreground is a classic Saarinen Tulip design, and the chairs are early models of the Eameses' iconic molded-fiberglass chairs. Dry mortar bags by Fiona Banner are both works of art and pillows.

A MOMENT OF LIFE CONCRETELY AND DELIBERATELY CONSTRUCTED

FRANCIS BACON
CATALOGUE RAISONNÉ

Le Corbusier

SCARPA

Top • Home office shelves are lined with a collection of design and art books on Yantrasast's favorite topics, including Duchamp, Matisse, and Le Corbusier.

Above • A note from an artist friend's grateful daughter, who swims in Yantrasast's pool.

Right • Yantrasast's home office is chock full of architectural models, mementos, and knickknacks.

A Marcel Wanders Knotted Chair finds
a home in the sleek master bath.

Above • Thick industrial felt curtains, a simple box spring bed, and a Chippensteel 0.5 Chair by Oskar Zięta comprise the minimalist master bedroom. A miniature version of the first coat Martin Margiela designed was created to commemorate Maison Margiela's twenty-fifth anniversary.

Overleaf • The three-story concrete, glass, and steel house makes the most of a postage stamp–size lot. The master bedroom extends out over an outdoor seating area on the pool level, and a "widow's walk" made of polycarbonate panels offers a sweeping view of Venice.

ARGYLE FARM

HUTTON AND RUTH WILKINSON'S RANCH, set in splendid isolation in the Santa Monica Mountains, is a Shangri-La if ever there was one. Boney Peak, said to have healing energy, rises to the north; to the west, the Channel Islands float in the Pacific.

Reached by a snaking dirt road off the Pacific Coast Highway, the 100-acre compound, an enclave of pagodas, pavilions, studios, and houses, the interiors of which are a pastiche of opulence and eccentricity, speaks to Wilkinson's thirty years working with Tony Duquette, the visionary Hollywood set designer turned interior designer. Wilkinson first came across Duquette's work in an article in the *Los Angeles Times Home Magazine* when he was in seventh grade. "I wanted to work with him from that moment on," says Wilkinson, who landed a job with Duquette at age seventeen. Over the course of their thirty-year collaboration, Wilkinson helped conceive many of the twentieth century's most storied houses for such illustrious clients as Vincente Minnelli, Doris Duke, Mary Pickford, J. Paul Getty, David O. Selznick, the Duchess of Windsor, and Dodie Rosekrans. Upon Duquette's death in 1999, Wilkinson purchased his mentor's share of the business. In addition to running Tony Duquette Studios, Wilkinson continues to design furniture, fabrics, tabletops, lighting, fireplaces, and bedding under the Duquette name.

It is hard to imagine Wilkinson relaxing—he's currently designing a hotel in Bangkok, taking advantage of intercontinental flights to write design and children's books—but if he does, it's here at Argyle Farm, which he and Ruth refer to as "a cross between Tobacco Road and San Simeon." Here, all decorating precepts are dismissed in favor of a magpie assortment of exotic objects, resulting in an ambience of extravagance, wit, and sheer artistry.

Duquette and Wilkinson embraced repurposing long before it became fashionable, and everything at Argyle Farm has a backstory. A pavilion near the entrance is from MGM studios, where it was used in a movie starring Debbie Reynolds and Glen Ford for which Duquette designed the set. "They were bulldozing the back lot and said we could

Opposite • In one of the living rooms at Argyle Farm, the sofas are covered in embroidered linen from India. A brass Moroccan brazier rests on an antique red lacquer coffee table from Japan. To the left of the stone fireplace hangs an oil painting by Elizabeth Duquette, wife of iconic designer Tony Duquette, who designed the chandelier. The miniature chair is from the collection of Shirley Temple.

Above • Panels from antique Coromandel screens hang on the walls in the master bedroom. The bronze palm-tree lamp is one of a pair flanking the bed.

have anything we wanted except the Esther Williams swimming pool, which we would have taken if we could have gotten it out of the ground," Wilkinson recalls.

The living room of the main house includes a massive chandelier from Buffums' bridal department, purchased when the upscale store went bankrupt. A Chippendale-style Chinese bed was made for the family of Jennie Jerome Churchill and eventually landed in the collection of New York decorator Harrison Cultra. Wilkinson's clients and friends Rucky and Leslie Barclay purchased the bed from Cultra's estate as a gift for the Huttons. "If that bed could talk, it would scream," swears Wilkinson. A red iron pagoda was fashioned out of an elevator car from the old Hollywood Hotel. "Tony turned it into the pagoda and put it on my property. We still serve lunch there." Duquette's own ranch was next door, but when it burned to the ground in the so-called Green Meadow fire of 1990, Wilkinson insisted that his mentor move into a guesthouse on their property, "I told him we couldn't be happy living out here unless he was there too."

Days at the ranch are immersive, if more subdued than the exotic surroundings might suggest. Mornings are spent hiking, playing tennis, and swimming. Lunch guests are often treated to Chinese chicken salad and Wilkinson's famous tamale pie. "It's always lunch, never dinner, and we serve more iced tea than wine because of the treacherous drive home." At night, countless stars light up the inky sky; only nature can outshine this otherworldly setting.

The red-walled library/guest room features a French daybed, an antique Oushak carpet, a mix of French and English antiques, and a smattering of painted Indian trunks and accessories. The painting over the daybed is by Elizabeth Duquette.

Presiding over the eat-in-country kitchen is an eighteenth-century carved wooden stag with real antlers found in an Austrian hunting lodge. A quilted-chintz throw covers the sofa. The carpet is woven raffia. Hanging above an eighteenth-century French chair are antique Chinese reverse paintings on glass. The iron chandelier is in the style of Diego Giacometti.

Left • In the master bedroom, the bed is a nineteenth-century Chinese Chippendale extravaganza topped by a little man in a boat. The walls are painted imperial yellow and hung with panels from antique Coromandel screens in red lacquered frames. The armoire and the red lacquered armchairs are a modern Chinese Chippendale design.

Above • A white porcelain chinoiserie stove completes the room's exotic theme.

Above • The walls of this guesthouse are trimmed in a blue-and-white Indian print and embedded with blue-and-white ceramic vases. The blue-and-white-tiled panel and the needlework rug are antique Portuguese. American Federal beds were painted white.

Opposite • An elaborately carved antique Indian arch forms the entrance to the blue-and-white bathroom. Tony Duquette designed the pair of pagodas flanking the bathroom door.

Opposite • Paths leading to the main house, outbuildings, and swimming pool are paved in flagstone.

Right • The main house at Argyle Farm was designed by AcademyAward–winning art director Lyle Wheeler for Henry Chamberlin in the 1940s.

Below • At the lagoon-like swimming pool, steps leading up to the diving platform are constructed out of boulders. Boney Peak, sacred to the native Chumash Indians, is visible in the distance.

Above • This pagoda was originally constructed in the 1950s by Tony Duquette out of an elevator cage from the old Hollywood Hotel. Hutton Wilkinson later acquired metal doors from the same hotel and raised the elevator cage up a flight to create a ground-level space now used for alfresco lunches.

Right • Indian statues flank the entrance to the upper guesthouse, which the Wilkinsons gave to Tony Duquette after his ranch next door was destroyed by fire. "Before we knew what was happening, Tony Duquette had constructed temples and gates and platforms, as well as an entire interior in gold lamé," says Wilkinson.

Overleaf • Duquette decorated the roof of a dining pavilion with spires made of old television satellite dishes and upside-down fence posts from Home Depot.

Left • The living room in Tony Duquette's guesthouse includes an African textile mounted as a wall hanging, a mirror surrounded by antique Chinese carvings, a woven wool rug, a club chair upholstered in denim, and a Thai spirit house atop Mexican wedding chests.

Below • In Tony Duquette's bedroom, Indian cotton prints are mounted on the walls and Southeast Asian carvings hang above the bed and on the doors. The framed painting is Indian, as is the mural of horses above the bed. The carpet is Moroccan.

Opposite • The terrace near the bedroom features paneling from Bali, a ceiling from Thailand, and statues and chairs from India, all framing Tony Duquette's *Phoenix Rising from Its Flames* sculpture, created in response to the fire that destroyed his nearby ranch.

EDWARDS HOUSE

ASK ANN PHILBIN HOW LONG SHE'S LIVED in Los Angeles and, like most transplants, she appears surprised at how swiftly the years have added up, but readily concedes, "This is home now." A logical conclusion, considering that in 1999, when Philbin moved here to become director of the Hammer Museum, it was as if the town was waiting for her. L.A. was bursting with cultural opportunities, which Philbin wholeheartedly embraced by inviting emerging artists as well as a roster of performers, filmmakers, authors, and advocacy groups to make the Hammer their home, transforming the once dormant institution into a vibrant multidisciplinary community center. "I had a vision of what it could be."

Philbin also admits to an obsession with design and construction. It's a passion that proved useful for refurbishing and expanding the Hammer and also came in handy when she and her partner, Cynthia Wornham, a California native, competitive surfer, and senior vice president of Strategic Engagement at Los Angeles's Natural History Museum, purchased the Edwards House, a 1957 minimalist post-and-beam affair by the powerhouse firm Buff, Straub & Hensman. As USC architecture professor Victor Regnier told the *Los Angeles Times* in 2002, "Almost every California architect educated since the early 1950s has been influenced by the work of Hensman, Buff and Straub, in one way or another." A point brought home when Philbin and Wornham's friend architect Frank Gehry visited the house and realized he had worked on its design while a USC architecture student.

Mindful of the house's pedigree, the couple embarked on a sensitive renovation under the guidance of architectural firm Chu + Gooding, specialists in modernist architecture. With the house restored and the kitchen and bathrooms updated, the couple chose simple interiors that would keep the focus on the house's inherently beautiful bones and create a laid-back, California vibe. At the same time, they hung Philbin's collection of works on paper, some by artist

Opposite • The 1957 minimalist post-and-beam Edwards House by the mid-century modern firm Buff, Straub & Hensman was gently restored by owners Ann Philbin and Cynthia Wornham under the guidance of architect Annie Chu, whom Philbin calls "a modernist house whisperer." Over the fireplace is a work by Lee Bontecou. Nineteenth-century Japanese vessels, a birthday gift from Agnes Gund to Ann, decorate a pair of coffee tables.

Above • A hummingbird nest, found on a branch in the garden, is displayed in a vintage water jug.

Top and above • A sweetgum tree shades the entrance walkway, which was restored according to a vintage Julius Shulman photograph.

Opposite • Philbin and Wornham painted the exterior of the front doors red, replicating the color of doors they had admired on a trip to Japan.

friends from her days as director of New York's Drawing Center and others by artists she met in L.A., including Kara Walker, Mark Grotjahn, Lari Pittman, Analia Saban, Mark Bradford, Barry McGee, Margaret Kilgallen, Robert Overby, and Robert Gober.

As the interiors bleed into the exteriors, the couple conceived a landscape design that would celebrate the house's elegant simplicity, reclaiming what they considered a coyote highway. "Now we can see the magnificent melaleuca trees," which were there but hidden by a ficus hedge. "We just added a fire pit designed by landscape architect Lisa Gimmy." The house is an expressive living space that not only telegraphs the impeccably good taste of its owners and perfectly reflects their sleek yet earthy aesthetic but also confirms Philbin's attachment to L.A.

Overleaf • In the living room, the sofa on the left was created by Suzanne Shaker, a New York designer and Philbin's dear friend. An iconic Eames Lounge Chair and Ottoman face the fireplace. To the left of the fireplace, Analia Saban's sculpture *Bag with Canvas* sits next to a work by Mark Bradford. The coffee tables are vintage Japanese.

Above • The dining table is surrounded by Saarinen chairs.

Opposite top left • A George Nelson Cigar Bubble wall sconce hangs in the master bedroom. Over the bed is a drawing by Los Angeles artist Robert Overby.

Opposite top right • A hallway leads from the living and dining areas to the bedroom. There is not a single step in the one-story house.

Opposite bottom • Philbin's office is furnished with a Mies van der Rohe Barcelona chair and a Florence Knoll desk. From left to right, the works on the wall are by Matt Lipps, Cindy Sherman, and Nick Herman.

Above • Details of the pool patio and pool. The couple's yellow Lab puppy, Olive, lies on a sofa designed by Suzanne Shaker (top left). The pool was rebuilt based on vintage photographs by Julius Shulman.

Right • Philbin designed a long bench to enclose the pool area and provide maximum seating when entertaining.

Below • The garden's design centers around the melaleuca trees.

Overleaf • The living room, kitchen, dining area, and master bedroom all open onto the pool. The house won an AIA award in 1959.

BUNGALOWS

THOUGH A BUNGALOW MAY SEEM WORLDS away from the stereotypical Tinseltown dwelling, the examples on the following pages prove that small is often the bold choice. Size hardly determines style, nor does it limit design opportunities. These enchanting residences share many traits with their grander neighbors: foyers, dining rooms, beamed ceilings, bedroom wings, glass walls, water features, and even miniature guesthouses, all designed with space-saving efficiency and ingenuity.

For a bungalow in the Silver Lake neighborhood, modernist Richard Neutra performed nothing short of sleight of hand, endowing the 1,300-square-foot residence with three bedrooms, enormous glass walls, and a courtyard. Designer Madeline Stuart's Spanish Revival combines the romance of a casita with the charm of an English cottage and looks out on an enchanting garden brimming with potted plants. Every inch of painter Don Bachardy's bungalow is covered with the work of fellow California artists, the whole of which is greater than the sum of its parts. The front door, merely steps from the beach, opens onto an intimate living room with a panoramic view of the Santa Monica Canyon; this storied bungalow is truly a classic California getaway.

Artist's Palette

Ask any Santa Monica local where Don Bachardy lives, and they'll point you down the hill toward an unprepossessing house overlooking Santa Monica Canyon where the artist has resided and worked since the 1960s, for many years with his late companion, the famed English writer Christopher Isherwood. Chris and Don, as they were known, were considered creative royalty; Bachardy painted portraits of Hollywood luminaries while Isherwood

Opposite • Painter Don Bachardy's Santa Monica bungalow is covered in art, much of it by fellow California artists. Among those whose works appear in this one area of his living room are Peter Alexander, Tom Wudl, Paul Wonner, Peter Lodato, Peter Zecher, Phyllis Green, Carole Caroompas, Chuck Arnoldi Gwynn Murrill, Eric Amouyal, Astrid Preston, Jessie Homer French, and Theophilus Brown.

Above • A study for Bachardy's official portrait of Governor Edmund Gerald "Jerry" Brown, 1983.

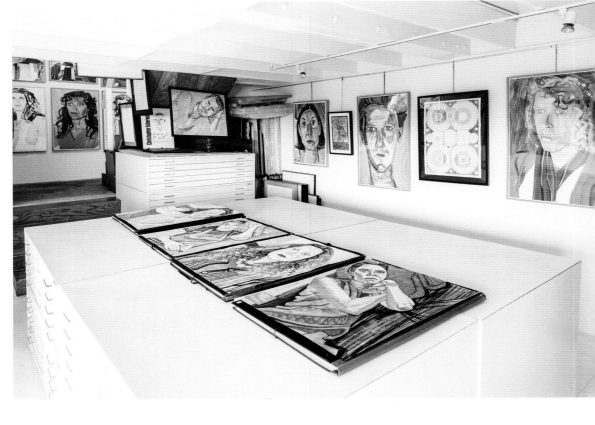

Above left • A walkway leads down a twisting path to the front door.

Above right and opposite • Portraits by Bachardy hang in his studio, where he paints daily. Subjects include Samantha Eggar, Alan Cumming, and Tony Bill. David Hockney's study of Bachardy and Isherwood hangs on the wall (opposite top left). The final painting, which was included in the 2017–18 retrospective of Hockney's work in Paris, New York, and London, can been seen in the open book beneath one of Bachardy's portraits of Isherwood (opposite bottom right).

wrote *The Berlin Stories*, the basis for *Cabaret*, as well as *A Single Man*, inspired by the couple's brief breakup and the subject of Tom Ford's film by the same name.

Isherwood and Bachardy met at the beach in the early 1960s. "I was little Donny from Atwater. After we started living together, this was our fifth house within walking distance of the ocean. We would get up at 7, work until 10:30, go to the ocean, eat lunch, and return to our workrooms until supper. It was a perfect life," Bachardy says.

Igor Stravinsky was one of Bachardy's first models, but his most devoted subject was Isherwood, and portraits of him still hang in every room of the cozy bungalow with its Spanish tile floors and art-covered, whitewashed walls. They socialized with Montgomery Clift, Ginger Rogers, Laurence Olivier, Bette Davis, Fred Astaire—all of whom would eventually pose for Bachardy. Many of the portraits are included in two of Bachardy's books, *Stars in My Eyes* (2000) and *Hollywood* (2014). "Marlene Dietrich came out. She was so sophisticated. She wore pedal pushers and a canvas hat, no makeup, as casual as could be. She eventually sat for me." More recently, Tilda Swinton, Marion Cotillard, Glenn Close, and Angelina Jolie have posed for him.

Bachardy continues to paint every day, rising with the sun and reading quietly until half past noon, when he has lunch. He then retreats to the same studio he and Isherwood built over their garage in 1976. "Christopher was the first person to think of me as an artist, and ever since he sent me to art school, I've felt obligated to really try. I think I've exceeded his expectations."

Overleaf • In this view of the living room, looking toward the dining room, the art includes works by Ed Ruscha, Jessie Homer French, Joe Fay, Ken Price, Phyllis Green, Joe Goode, Peter Alexander, Billy Al Bengston, Nancy Riegelman, Chuck Arnoldi, and Keith Vaughan, who was Bachardy's teacher at the Slade School of Fine Art in London.

Left and below • The dining room table was acquired from set designer and interior decorator Tony Duquette, for whom Bachardy once worked. The art in the dining room includes works by Tom Wudl, Billy Al Bengston, and Ned Evans.

Opposite • In the kitchen, high above the Wedgewood stove, are photos of the historian and philosopher Gerald Heard, and over the doorway is an ear painting by Jessie Homer French. The large painting over the stove is by Eric Amouyal. The colorful bowls on the counter are by Phyllis Green.

Left • Bachardy's bedroom has a sweeping view of Santa Monica Canyon. A photo of his late companion, writer Christopher Isherwood, is displayed on the headboard.

Above • The work above the bathroom scale is by Karla Klarin.

Passion Play

When Maroon 5 bassist Mickey Madden began outgrowing a modernist Craig Ellwood house, he did what he and his bandmates do whenever they have questions of aesthetics. He called L.A.'s style sorcerer, Mark Haddawy, who has made a living anticipating what people want and then exceeding their expectations. A thrift-store junkie, Haddawy and his business partner, Katy Rodriguez, founded Resurrection, a series of vintage clothing boutiques that transformed yesterday's duds into aspirational collectibles. His transition to interior design was equally organic and prescient. Friend and photographer Mark Seliger so admired Haddawy's restoration of his own home, Pierre Koenig's Case Study House #21, that he hired Haddawy to transform his Richard Neutra house, and another career was born. "I've been into mid-century modern for over thirty years. I've watched Design Within Reach become a thing," says Haddawy, who has since restored four Neutras and two Lautners for clients including director Marc Forster, fashion designer Jeremy Scott, and nearly every member of Maroon 5. Now he's putting his own stamp on the L.A. landscape, building projects from the ground up.

"Aside from more space, Mickey wanted something warmer, with layering, texture. The Ellwood house has a more austere aesthetic and we couldn't get there." The answer was right up the street in a 1960 Edward H. Fickett modernist design with Craftsman influences. Fickett is best known for the more than 60,000 homes he designed, known as "Fickett Houses." In deference to the architecture, Haddawy chose chairs by George Nakashima, Arne Norell, and Vico Magistretti, while providing moodier layering with lush velvet curtains and royal blue sofas.

Haddawy applied the same principle to the garden. "Mickey wanted it to feel rich, not too arid." Mondo grass and fern-like *Phoenix roebelenii* augment Haddawy's favorite indigenous plants, including agave, yucca, and a variety of palm trees, continuing the nuanced combination of a modern backdrop laced with warm touches. "I pull it together, but Mickey has a real sense of what he's into. It's Mickey's world—he's very connected to his surroundings."

Madden keeps abreast of interior design the same way he does music. "I listen to everything under the sun, going down rabbit hole on the internet and digging through record stores in both L.A. and New York. I've educated myself about furniture the same way, going on 1st Dibs to learn the values of things and perusing local dealers."

Opposite • The entrance to musician Mickey Madden's 1960s Ed Fickett house, with interiors by Mark Haddawy, includes a George Nakashima chair and a painting by Mathew Cerletty.

Above • The library is furnished with a table and chairs by Adrian Pearsall and a Pierre Chapo daybed.

Overleaf • Brazilian sofas anchor the living room, where Pierre Chapo Dromedary chairs sit on a vintage Serapi rug. The print over the fireplace is by Sigmar Polke. The skylight, beams, and finishes are all original.

Left • The kitchen cabinets are original to the house.

Below • In the dining area, the table and chairs are by Afra and Tobia Scarpa. The painting on the far wall is by Genieve Figgis, and the photos on the freestanding wall are by Bruce Nauman.

Opposite • In the brick-lined library, Mickey Madden's prized Rickenbacker 4003 bass guitar leans against a bookcase.

Above • A Gibson EB-2 bass guitar sits on an Arne Norell Sirocco Safari chair in a corner of the master bedroom. The portrait of Brian Jones is by an unknown photographer.

Opposite • Vico Magistretti chairs, a vintage Caucasian rug, and cotton velveteen curtains combine with the brick fireplace and warm wood floor to create the master bedroom's inviting and soothing atmosphere.

A boldly wallpapered guest room features a vintage desk and an Aldo Tura bar cart.

To implement Mickey Madden's vision of a garden for his mid-ceneury modern house that felt "rich, not too arid," Haddaway enlisted Mayo Casiano to plant indigenous succulents such as *Dracaena, Agave Attenuata,* and aloe.

California Bountiful

The minute she arrived from Pittsburgh in the 1990s to study critical theory in Pasadena's ArtCenter Graduate Art MFA program, gallerist Sarah Gavlak was spellbound by Los Angles, "It seemed so exotic. I picked oranges from the trees and lived in this amazing mid-century modern house in Silver Lake. It was just so hopeful and optimistic," she says. A burgeoning career as an art writer and an independent curator drew her back to the East Coast, but twenty years later she answered L.A.'s siren song again and opened a gallery in Hollywood. "There's so much opportunity and potential here. Artists are making a path for themselves. It's exciting to be a part of that."

Gavlak's first order of business was to find a home in which she, her husband, and their young son would feel firmly rooted. Without any particular architectural style in mind, the lifelong devotee of architecture and design knew something would speak to her. Inspiration struck in the form of a breezy 1941 classic California ranch. Gavlak decorated it with an idiosyncratic assemblage of contemporary art, mid-century modern pieces, and Hollywood Regency–style furniture, which has appealed to her puckish spirit all her life. "I adore the idea of an eighteenth-century bergère chair juxtaposed with a Joan Mitchell painting."

Gavlak found most of the furniture off the beaten path, shopping at thrift shops and flea markets. "I was building my business and putting all of my money into art, so I learned to spot a deal. Jane Holzer and Beth DeWoody are huge supporters, and I watched how they've put things together with finds from the Paris and Florida flea markets. It was a real education. The great news is that with contemporary there aren't rules."

The mix-and-match décor communicates the joy she experienced when she first arrived in Los Angeles. "I have coffee outside in the morning and in the evening we smell orange blossoms. It's just so appealing."

Below • Green velvet sofas with Lucite legs are a nod to Gavlak's love of Hollywood Regency. A photograph by David Haxton hangs to the right of a ceramic vessel by Elisabeth Kley. The work over the mantel is a Jose Alvarez collage from his series *The Awakening*. A Mies van der Rohe Barcelona daybed sits in a windowed corner.

Opposite • A large knitted banner by Lisa Anne Auerbach dominates the dining room. Chairs that Gavlak found in Palm Beach and recovered in a zebra velvet surround a custom dining table. The Shoji decanter and glasses by Imperial Glass date to the 1960s.

Right • In her study, Gavlak recovered the seat of a brass Chiavari chair in pink velvet, her favorite color. The coffee table is vintage Italian. The art includes a Marilyn Minter photograph, a drawing by Andrew Brischler, and a ceramic piece by Brian Rochefort. The pink poodle magazine holder was a gift from collector Beth DeWoody.

Below • In the master bedroom, a collage by T. J. Wilcox hangs over the mantel. The table in the window bay is Biedermeier.

Urban Zen

Susan Nimoy and her late husband, actor Leonard Nimoy, purchased their Bel Air house in 1987 and immediately set about quieting the interiors. Moldings were removed, enormous windows and shiny dark wood floors were installed, and walls were painted a crisp white to show off couple's collection of works by female artists, including Kara Walker, Barbara Kruger, Lee Bontecou, and Louise Bourgeois.

The couple eventually discovered that their property included thousands of additional square feet of outdoor space, allowing them to build another small structure. In keeping with their minimalist leanings, they conceived a mediation room inspired by a Japanese teahouse. "I thought of it as Kyoto meets Axel Vervoordt," says Nimoy, referring to the Belgian designer renowned for creating austere but elegant atmospheres. "We wanted a sense of authenticity, so we used 400-year-old barn siding for the floor, bamboo for the pitched ceiling, and Japanese chandeliers. Holly Hunt had a dark fabric that we felt really captured the minimal feeling. We incorporated a drift-wood altar. For a time, it was our private spot to reflect."

Recently, Susan transformed the teahouse into a Red Tent room, in homage to Anita Diamant's novel about women's solidarity, for a dinner with female friends. "We had a crowning ceremony and a candlelight dinner with two tables of multigenerational women from the literary world, filmmaking, politics—all my female soul mates."

A pool with slate coping and edged by a bamboo stand creates a serene setting for the meditation room that Susan and the late Leonard Nimoy built when they discovered thousands of square feet of additional outdoor space on their Bel Air property.

Opposite • The pool's fountain generates the soothing sound of moving water.

Right and below • Inspired by a Japanese teahouse, the structure has a pitched roof and Japanese chandeliers. The floorboards are 400-year-old barn siding. An altar was crafted from driftwood.

Perfectly Imperfect

A good part of interior designer Madeline Stuart's genius is a cast-off elegance that renders her work inimitable. Though she takes a more exacting approach when fulfilling a client's mandate, her own house is at once urbane and bohemian, combining the romance of a Spanish casita with the alluring elements of a charming English cottage, including an enchanting garden brimming with potted plants.

"I've never set out to create a 'look' for this house," she says. "I bring furniture in and out. Some pieces have been around for ages, and there are things I know I should change, but I just haven't gotten around to them. I love my bed, but if we're being completely honest, it's a showroom sample from my furniture collection that I dragged home a few years ago. I've painted my living room six times in seventeen years and I'm still not happy about the color. And I keep meaning to build out the spare bedroom so it can be a fabulous auxiliary closet, but I've yet to do so. I pay far less attention to my own home than I probably should."

If the interiors are forever evolving, Stuart is disinclined to tamper with the structure. Having grown up in a Beverly Hills Spanish Revival house with exceptional detailing, she's a natural champion of the style. "Everything about my childhood house influenced my reverence for Spanish Revival and Mediterranean architecture. So many homes dating from the 1930s have been mutilated by inappropriate remodeling and the type of 'modernization' that completely disrespects the architecture."

A restorationist at heart, Stuart set about remodeling the kitchen and her closet with cabinetry consistent with the kind that would have been installed when the house was built. She stripped paint, stained the wood floors, and installed vintage lighting. "I didn't do anything to the bathrooms, as they were in great shape. They have the original tile work, and the color combinations, mauve and black, as well as Ming green and black, are quite striking."

When she and her husband, writer Steve Oney, purchased the house seventeen years ago, they planned to stay about five years and move on, "but we still love our little house." So she continues tinkering, collecting and culling inherited and repurposed objects and furniture. It changes, but it remains the same—it's impossible to improve upon the perfectly imperfect.

Opposite • Creeping fig and Boston ivy crown the front gate of designer Madeline Stuart's Spanish Revival bungalow.

Below left and right • Maintaining a boxwood garden augmented with varieties of *Pittosporum* "requires an Edward Scissorhands!" Stuart declares. The outdoor furniture is vintage John Salterini and John Good.

Overleaf • In the living room, two chairs designed by Stuart are covered in Fortuny silk velvet, and a pair of eighteenth-century Danish bergères is upholstered in a Rogers & Goffigon linen. The iron-and-leather chairs are vintage Italian. A vintage convex mirror and a bear skull are set in a niche over the fireplace, which is original to the house.

Left • Hanging to the left of the archway leading from the living room to Stuart's home office are sixteenth- and seventeenth-century Spanish and Iznik tiles from the collection of Lockwood de Forest. The round, slate-topped table to the right is nineteenth-century French. The alabaster lamp is from the 1940s.

Below • Mr. Peabody and Beatrice sit on the sofa in the living room. Stuart designed the scored-brass coffee table with a lacquered cracked-linen top.

Opposite • The banister and lantern are original to the house, built in 1930. On the landing, a nineteenth-century cane-backed English chair sits next to a Chinese root table.

Left • Stuart designed the shutters for what was originally an open-air sleeping porch. The sofa is covered in a Raoul Textiles fabric.

Below • Golden wool sateen curtains contrast with the dining room's lavender walls. A French eglomise mirror dates to the 1940s.

Top left • Stuart left the bathroom in its original state, complete with nineteenth-century Portuguese tiles and 1930s fittings.

Bottom left • The walls of Stuart's dressing room are hand painted in a design inspired by Dagobert Peche. Stuart designed the vanity. The chandelier is 1940s French, and the chair is nineteenth-century Italian.

Above • Stuart designed the bed in the master bedroom. The chair is Austrian, the bench is French, and the lamps are Japanese. A small work by Darren Waterston hangs over the bed.

Neutra Revisited

In 1932 budding modernist architect Richard Neutra created a home on a tiny sliver of land along the water in Silver Lake, an artistic hub then as it is now. Employing natural light and glass walls that opened onto patio gardens and working with a budget of only $10,000, he considered it a deft experiment in urban living that would prove modern innovations were not limited to affluent clients.

A stone's throw from Neutra's original experiment, on a quiet block cantilevered over Silver Lake, sits a subsequent articulation of it. Built in 1959, the 1,300-square-foot residence serves as an eloquent reminder that a small living space can not only employ good design but also deliver a stylish family home. "Neutra's designs don't necessarily get any better the bigger they get," says owner and interior designer David Netto. "The finishes in all of his houses are very humble: linoleum, plywood, that kind of thing."

Netto originally purchased the house as a West Coast base for himself and his first daughter, Kate. "We had very little furniture and piles of Legos and it was really very enjoyable," he says. Eventually, when his second daughter, Madeline, was born and Netto and his wife, Liz, relocated to L.A., he set about transforming the house into a primary residence for the family of four. "I hired my friend Paul Fortune to collaborate on the house, as I thought it would be easier on our marriage to have a third party involved."

Within three meetings, Fortune and Netto veered deliberately off course, creating an unexpected scheme. Adventurous by nature, Netto explains, "I've seen beautifully done Neutra houses restored as case studies. But I wanted to add to the canon of how people live in these glass houses. Before modernism calcified into doctrine, you saw modernist buildings filled with rococo, African furniture and rugs—there wasn't a manifesto. I was excited about being unleashed in California and I didn't want to undershoot."

Netto's straight aim resulted in informal interiors that hardly feel at odds with the house's minimalist design. Rather, the décor is more along the lines of European modernism in its mix of vintage, antique, and mid-century furniture and art of varying pedigrees and eras. An indication of the house's success lies in the fact it has a leading role in Nancy Meyer's film *The Holiday*, confirming what Netto's devotees already knew: there is something unique in his outlook. But the real triumph is thanks to the insouciant air that he and Liz bring to the place. "After all, this is a family home and we use every inch. For that, we had to banish perfection," he says.

Left and opposite • A courtyard entrance, a signature of modernist architect Richard Neutra, connects the carport and the master bedroom. The chairs are from Janus et Cie.

Overleaf • Built in 1959, the 1,300-square-foot residence sits on a quiet block cantilevered over Silver Lake. The addition of a reflecting pool remains faithful to the spirit of Neutra's designs.

Above • Netto furnished the house with mid-century modern pieces, including Poul Kjaerholm PK 15 chairs, a Jean Prouvé table by Vitra, and a Diego Giacometti standing lamp from Galerie L'Arc en Seine.

Opposite • In the living room, barrel chairs are 1920s Austrian from JF Chen. A Jean-Michel Frank rock crystal lamp sits on a palmwood table by Pierre Chareau.

Overleaf • Madeline Netto and Dusty in the family's 1997 Bentley Brooklands.

SIMPLICITY AND SPACE

MENTION TO ANY ARTISTICALLY INCLINED

Angeleno that you're en route to Margo Leavin's house, and the reaction is likely to be, "Can I join you?" Such interest is understandable, as Leavin's gallery on Robertson Boulevard, founded in 1970, was a cornerstone for the dealers, curators, and artists who eventually transformed L.A. into a world-class art hub. Until the gallery closed in 2013, she mounted more than four hundred solo shows for the likes of John Baldessari, Claes Oldenburg, Lynda Benglis, Joseph Kosuth, Sol LeWitt, Donald Judd, and William Leavitt.

Not one to flaunt her accomplishments, during a visit Leavin steers the conversation away from her storied career, focusing instead on the house to which she was drawn from the first moment she saw it in 1982. "It felt very airy walking in." Reputed to be methodical and deliberate, Leavin returned ten times to confirm that the residence checked all the design boxes in her head. Its sliding pocket doors created cross ventilation and blurred the boundary between inside and outside. A gracious main floor would accommodate monthly artists' dinners, and a terraced garden, originally laid out by Emmet Wemple, had been neglected but held great promise and had sweeping views. "Coming home from the gallery location on Robertson, I appreciated the serene vista."

Still, the prospect of running a business and simultaneously renovating a house gave Leavin pause. "What convinced me I could do it was the fact that the house came equipped with superbly constructed built-in bookcases, desks, dressers, benches, and four fireplaces—I've never lived without a fireplace," she says.

The house was built in 1941 for oil producer and philanthropist G. Allan Hancock by USC architect C. Raimond Johnson. Leavin wanted to update it but not amend its restrained beauty. She recruited architect and friend David Serrurier, who she knew would preserve the structure's simplicity and spaciousness. Together they carried out the painstaking restoration of original fixtures and woodwork, which proved an effective backdrop for Leavin's personal collection. "Art placement is very intuitive, very difficult to explain," she says. "Depending on the wall you choose for a

Opposite • Gary Stephan's *Untitled*, 1980, hangs above a black lacquer table and armchair by Josef Hoffmann, ca. 1902, in a breezeway in legendary art dealer Margo Leavin's home, designed by C. Raimond Johnson in 1941.

Above • An avid reader, Margo Leavin keeps her favorite tomes on hand in the study.

Above · Leavin painted the house's exterior terra-cotta to give it a Mediterranean look.

Right · Leavin worked with architect David Serrurier to gently restore the house's finishes. In the entrance hall, Claes Oldenburg's *3-Way Plug, Scale C, Soft*, 1970, is displayed in a Plexiglas case, and a small sculpture by John Chamberlain, *Tonk #15*, 1986, rests on the ledge at the base of the paldao wood staircase.

Opposite · Marcel Breuer chairs surround a custom-made dining table. Hanging on the wall above the console is an untitled 1977 work by Jasper Johns. To the right is Joseph Kosuth's *Double Reading #24*, 1993. On the wall in the adjoining living room is Lynda Benglis's sprayed-aluminum *Alpha II*, 1975.

work, it demands your attention differently." She hung a work by John Baldessari that is composed of several images on a long horizontal wall. A larger piece by Lynda Benglis benefited from being positioned so that it could be seen from across the room. She chose a beloved Martin Puryear sculpture to hang over one of the fireplaces.

Leavin turned to garden designer Richard Naranjo, noted for his work on the Getty Villa and Getty Center, to reclaim the grounds, which now include a hill of cedars, a small citrus grove, and a year-round vegetable bed. At various phases she has also consulted landscape architects Pamela Burton and Lisa Moseley. "Since my office is now at home, I've had more time to devote to and enjoy the gardens," says Leavin. To make the house resonate with the Mediterranean feeling of her prized garden, in a surprising flourish Leavin painted it terra-cotta, going so far as to carry home a brick of the precise color from Italy. The house stands proudly at the top of its street, rising like a palazzo in a Tuscan hill town, raising curiosity in all who see it from afar, and transporting anyone lucky enough to enter.

Above • Yves Klein's painted-plaster *La Victoire de Samothrace*, 1962, stands on a cabinet near Leavin's desk.

Right • In the center of the study is a vellum coffee table with a black glass top by architect Marcello Piacentini, ca. 1930. Roy Dowell's *Untitled (#691)*, 1996, hangs over Allen Ruppersberg's *Al's Grand Hotel Artifacts*, 1996. To the right is an untitled 1946 work by Ad Reinhardt.

John Baldessari's silver gelatin print *Three Tires and a Chinese Man*, 1984, hangs at the top of the staircase.

Left • Claes Oldenburg's *Alphabet/Good Humor*, 1975.

Below • A Cy Twombly inscribed offset lithograph, 1981, hangs over Alan Belcher's *Velcro Attache*, 1987.

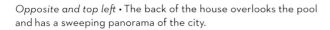

Opposite and top left • The back of the house overlooks the pool and has a sweeping panorama of the city.

Above left • A cluster of topiaried bushes surrounds a tree and softens a gravel-covered area of the garden.

Above right • Garden designer Richard Naranjo, along with landscape architects Pamela Burton and Lisa Moseley, reclaimed the grounds, which had long been neglected. The property now boasts a hill of cedars, a small citrus grove, and a year-round vegetable bed.

Overleaf • The outdoor furniture on a pergola-covered patio on one side of the house is from the Richard Schultz 1966 Collection.

ART DECO OPULENCE

JANE AND MARC NATHANSON WERE immediately attracted to a historic 1920s Art Deco villa designed by Lloyd Wright (Frank's son) not only for its glamour quotient, elegant proportions, and abundance of natural light but also for the opportunity it presented to display their collection of twentieth-century art. "In a past life I did interior design and I always liked the juxtaposition of old and new, so I knew our Pop Art would look wonderful here," says Jane Nathanson.

After raising three children in the house, the Nathansons upped the art ante, calling upon interior designer Richard Hallberg to replace a moldering addition with a new one that could serve as a gallery. The process and result proved so pleasing that it had a domino effect and before long, clients and designer were inching their way through the house, revamping the entire first floor and garden to correspond to the new addition. "We weren't really going to do anything but the addition," Nathanson remembers. "The rest of the house just unfolded."

Hallberg's aim was to simplify and unify the main house and the addition, giving the entire residence a quiet cohesion. To that end, the addition's oval entrance hall echoes the home's curved foyer. The gallery on the addition's lower floor features polished-concrete floors and plain white walls that enhance rotating installations of works by the likes of Andy Warhol, Frank Stella, Roy Lichtenstein, Dan Flavin, and Julian Schnabel.

The existing swimming pool was moved three feet, resulting in a more pleasing alignment with both the addition and the main house. Digging up the pool provided an opportunity to simplify the garden. Now its clean, contemporary combination of hedges and white hardscape showcases sculptures by Richard Serra and Alexander Calder. "I love flowers in the house, but I'm not much of a gardener. Green hedges are easy to care for and provide a perfect backdrop for sculpture," Nathanson says. The verdant green of the backyard creates a pleasing but stark contrast to the gleaming white entrance hall and the neutral palette of the living room.

Opposite • Jane and Marc Nathanson's 1920s Art Deco villa is an unexpected backdrop for a collection of twentieth-century art. Designer Richard Hallberg resurfaced the oval entrance hall in stone and stained the terrazzo staircase a dark gray. In the living room, a 1983 chromium-and-painted-steel sculpture by John Chamberlain hangs over a console with a tree-form base.

Above • A small stone obelisk and spheres top a table.

Right • The hallway leading from the entrance hall, past a sitting room, to the dining room features an untitled 1987 work by Donald Judd in the foreground, and George Segal's *Woman in Front of Corrugated Wall*, 1980. Neon spheres serve as decorative lighting.

Opposite top • The Donald Judd and George Segal works, seen from the sitting room.

Opposite bottom • Jeff Koons's *Balloon Rabbit Wall Relief*, 2008, hangs in the entrance hall to the left of the doorway to the living room.

Overleaf • From the top of the stairs in the entrance hall, Marc Sijan's *Security Guard Sylvester* overlooks Frank Stella's *La Colomba Ladra*, 1984.

Rather than play to type by selecting Art Deco furniture, Hallberg introduced an unexpected but harmonious mix of contemporary, classical, and above all cozy furnishings, including rattan chairs and antique consoles. "Life is more casual now and we want everyone to be comfortable." When surrounded by perfectly curated art, the result is a distinctive hybrid of restraint and exuberance.

Though perfectly appointed, in the end the house is about substance over style. Its importance lies in what unfolds there: a full schedule of fund raisers benefiting such organizations as the Los Angeles County Museum of Art, UCLA, the Pacific Council on International Policy, and the National Disability Institute. "But our favorite events are family dinners. When we moved here we had three children. Now we have eight grandchildren, so when we sit down to dinner, we're sixteen," says Nathanson, whose revised house, in the final analysis, is all about family.

Left and below • Andy Warhol's *Double Elvis*, 1963, and Ellsworth Kelly's *Yellow Black*, 1988, pop against the living room's ebonized-walnut floors and stark white plasterwork, a combination conceived by interior designer Richard Hallberg to allow the art to take center stage.

Opposite • Franz Kline's *Black and White #60*, 1960, hangs over the living room mantel. To the left is Andy Warhol and Jean-Michel Basquiat's *GE Tobacco Section*, 1984–85. A gilt console, from Therien & Co., adds a glamorous and, in this context, whimsical touch.

Above and right • The dining room features Roy Lichtenstein's *Woman with Peanuts*, 1962 (above), Pablo Picasso's *Tête d'homme*, 1971, and Damian Hirst's *Blue on Blue*, 2005, all illuminated by an eighteenth-century rock-crystal chandelier.

Opposite top • Ellsworth Kelly's *White and Green Curve*, 1978, and Roy Lichtenstein's *Vicki*, 1964, have found a home on one wall in the family room.

Opposite bottom • An untitled 1991 work by Donald Judd climbs another wall in the room. To the right is an untitled 1970 work by Cy Twombly. Barbara Kruger's *Untitled (The future belongs to those who can see it)*, 1993, hangs over the mantel.

Above • In the gallery addition, Hallberg covered the floor in sixteenth-century charcoal limestone to anchor the light-filled entrance hall, where Andy Warhol's *Self-Portrait (Shockwig)* and Alexander Calder's *Nine Discs of Which One Is Vertical*, greet guests.

Overleaf • "I find gray and white to be very soothing and neutral—neither too feminine nor masculine," says Jane Nathanson of the color scheme in the master bedroom, where Marlo Pascual's *Untitled*, a photograph with candle sconces, 2008–9, hangs above a desk.

Herb Ritts's photograph *Backflip, Paradise Cove*, 1987, hangs in the master bath.

Clockwise from above • A chest inlaid with mother-of-pearl; an untitled 1951 painting by Jackson Pollock over a settee; Melanie Pullen's *General Patton*, 2008, at the top of the stairs; detail of the deep gray fabric headboard in the master bedroom.

Left and opposite • A spacious and inviting veranda overlooks the garden and pool.

Below • Jane Nathanson collaborated with Richard Hallberg on the garden design. They opted for the clean lines of boxwood hedges as a backdrop for a 1963 Alexander Calder stabile.

RAW AND REFINED

IT'S NO SURPRISE THAT SOMEONE WHO cites Peggy Guggenheim and Doris Duke as style heroes flipped the script on interior design from the moment she unveiled one of her first projects in 1994. Beverly Hills' Avalon Hotel, furnished with a bold and bedazzling mix of neoclassic, Regency, and lacquer pieces, ushered in a new era in California living. Soon celebrities Gwen Stefani, Cameron Diaz, Ben Stiller, and Jeanne Tripplehorn asked Kelly Wearstler to inject a glamorous but free-spirited vibe into their private houses. A line of furnishings, a series of monographs, a commission to design Bergdorf Goodman's popular restaurant, BG, and a conceptualization of the interiors of the Viceroy Hotel chain followed. Dana Goodyear wrote in the *New Yorker* that Wearstler was "the presiding grande dame of West Coast interior design. . . . [She] represents the uninhibited side of Los Angeles, the part that celebrates how far the city is from strict East Coast notions of good taste."

Wearstler's style, like that of any true talent, evolves with every project. "My job as a designer is to be a good listener and to run my client's vision through my filter," she says. "It is still about translating distinctive personalities and finding a vibe." In the case of a Malibu beach house, the client was her family, and her mission was to create an alluring sanctuary on a broad, secluded stretch of beach. "It takes time to find the right home where the energy feels good. We knew this one was it. It has the most beautiful rock in the ocean right in front of the house. It is a sculpture from Mother Nature for us to enjoy every day."

Wearstler set about restyling the original house into a light-flooded, open-floor plan that she envisioned as a backdrop for interiors that would reflect the raw, unaffected surf culture of the 1970s. The tone is set in a breathtaking two-story atrium, where the sun streaming through a skylight illuminates a fifteen-foot ficus. "The lifestyle here is all about celebrating nature, health, and consciousness," she points out. "Therefore, nothing in the house is overly precious or fussed over. Malibu is chic and cool but also amazingly laid back. I wanted to echo that sensibility." Neutral colors such as deep

Opposite • To create an inviting family sanctuary on a secluded stretch of beach in Malibu, designer Kelly Wearstler channeled the raw, unaffected surf culture of the 1970s. In the living room, a vintage chaise and a table of bronze, glass, and steel by Silas Seandel rest on a Moroccan rug.

Above • A vintage vase was found in Palm Springs.

The entrance hall features a fabric wall hanging in the shape of a sea fan by Sheila Hicks.

blondes and creamy whites, and natural materials, including wood, marble, and stone, reflect the beach and absorb the ocean's changing hues. Furniture and objects evoke the idea of flotsam and jetsam: stools of petrified wood, light fixtures resembling seaweed, and a wall hanging by Sheila Hicks that suggests a sea fan.

The result is a soothing retreat that encourages all who enter to slow down and tune into nature. For Wearstler's family, a relaxing weekend means surfing, entertaining friends, watching movies, and at the end of each day, taking in the incredible sunsets over the Pacific. "Our days at the house are filled with love."

Above • Wearstler bought the vintage nautilus sculpture from Francis Sultana on 1stdibs.com. She found the painting, an unsigned work from the 1970s, in London. The stone pieces, ca. 1980s, are Paris flea market finds.

Overleaf • A low-slung, vintage Tobia Scarpa sofa, wood chairs by Lou Hodges, and metal cube chairs by Radboud Van Beekum for Pastoe surround a Gae Aulenti coffee table at one end of the living room. A 1970s geometric cabinet is from JF Chen. Enamel-and-glass table lamps dating to the 1970s were found in France.

Top • Vintage chaises longues separate the living area from the dining area.

Above and opposite • A stone-topped dining table, bought at auction, is surrounded by Zuma chairs from Wearstler's own furniture line. The art over the sideboard is from Pegaso Gallery Design, Los Angeles.

Above and opposite • The kitchen is swathed in Calacatta marble.
The banquette is covered in a Moore & Giles leather.

Left • A hanging textile in the game room is from a Paris flea market.

Below • A seating area features a leather collage from the 1970s. The sofas are covered in a Bob Collins & Sons fabric.

Opposite • The airy, open atmosphere of the house is established in the two-story atrium, where a fifteen-foot ficus thrives in the sunlight streaming in through a skylight. The rug is from Mansour.

Above • In the master dressing room, a sculpture purchased at a Paris flea market sits on a 1970s California table.

Opposite top left • A painting by Joshua Elias rests atop a custom-designed cabinet.

Opposite top right • The walls, floor, and bathtub in the master bath are covered in Bardiglio marble.

Opposite bottom • A 1970s Italian chaise sits between the master bath and bedroom. The black and white coloration of the bathroom marble is picked up in the lamp, end table, walls, rug, and artwork in the bedroom, including the black-and-white-checkered painting by Tofer Chin.

Opposite • A bathroom clad in tiger's-eye-patterned tile features a 1970s California chair.

Right • In a guest bedroom, the lifesize sculpture was purchased at auction. Vintage swivel chairs were reupholstered in a Larsen fabric.

Below • In another guest bedroom, a Medusa sculpture was transformed into a headboard.

Overleaf • The tide rolls in, dolphins and seals swim by, and the sunsets are breathtaking at Kelly Wearstler's family beach house in Malibu.

LYRICAL BEAUTY

"I THINK OF A HOME AS A VISUAL BIOGRAPHY," says fourth-generation Angeleno Oliver Furth, who learned a thing or two about design narrative while working for such top designers as Michael S. Smith, Martyn Lawrence Bullard, Trip Haenisch, and the late Greg Jordan before establishing his own firm. His clients include Arianna Huffington, Melissa Rivers, and a number of big players in the film and television industries.

The interiors of Furth's own house, a 1926 Spanish-style duplex in Carthay Circle, indicate that he likes to mix twentieth-century California furnishings with classic pieces and that his grandparents collected Danish modern furniture. A collection of heady objects reveals that he is the chairman emeritus of the Decorative Arts and Design Council at the Los Angeles County Museum of Art. "My house is a bit of a lab. I am constantly trying things here, where I'm not afraid of failure." What his space doesn't directly communicate is that at age nine, Furth already had his own subscription to *Architectural Digest* and that when he was a teen, his room was in shades of charcoal, black, and white.

Furth's youthful instincts foreshadowed a lifelong penchant for elegance and drama, which is fully on display in a client's splendid neo-Georgian house designed by classical architect Oscar Shamamian in Pacific Palisades. Furth wanted to respect the house's formality while rendering it warm and welcoming for a family with four rambunctious children and a congenial matriarch who leads a bustling social life.

A self-proclaimed old-fashioned modernist, Furth approached the traditional setting with a fresh outlook. "The owner said she wanted to live in poetry, something I always hold with me. Poetry is about saying the most by saying the least. I thought, we'll pay attention to the use of negative space." Setting such strict parameters from the beginning led Furth to the bold decision to decorate the cavernous space with fewer but more dramatic pieces, creating rare statements: eighteenth-century antiques read like sculptures and handsome window treatments

Opposite • An enormous jacaranda tree shades the garden entrance to this neo-Georgian house designed by Oscar Shamamian of Ferguson & Shamamian. Oliver M. Furth was responsible for the interiors.

Above • Boston ivy covers the wall of a small garden off the pool house.

have the sweep of ball gowns. Walls painted oyster react beautifully to the warm California light. "In another setting, the same color would feel dead and sad," he acknowledges.

As the client sits on environmental boards, Furth furnished the public rooms with intimate seating arrangements that can accommodate as few as two to as many as two hundred for cocktails. "I've been in those rooms wearing a tuxedo and I have also sat on the floor with the kids, and it all works," says Furth.

Several times a year on her extensive travels, the client will reach out to Furth with an inspiration. Most recently, the velvety green mountains of Switzerland suggested a new room color. "A great house is a living, breathing thing. This house is constantly evolving," says Furth.

Top • The planters flanking the front entrance are from Authentic Provence. They are reproductions of those designed by André Le Nôtre in the seventeenth century for the gardens of Versailles.

Above • A painting by Julian Schnabel hangs in the entrance hall. The stone table is from Quatrain, Los Angeles. The small sculpture of a hand is by the husband-and-wife team of François-Xavier and Claude Lalanne.

Above • A nineteenth-century Venetian mirror hangs over a neoclassical Swedish chest. The porcelain-and-steel table lamp was designed by Belgian sculptor and lighting designer Isabelle Farahnick.

Overleaf • In the sunroom, the sofas are covered in silk handwoven in Cambodia. The coffee table is antique Chinese, purchased at JF Chen. The chairs are by Michael S. Smith for his Jasper Collection.

Opposite • The delicate lacquered paneling that covers the dining room's walls is by Nancy Lorenz. The ceramic vessels on the nineteenth-century Regency console are by Ojai-based potter Chris Brock.

Above • An antique George III table anchors the dining room. The chairs are reproduction Georgian, upholstered in a vintage Fortuny striped cotton. In the bay window is a Jacob Kjær sofa. The handwoven raffia-and-cotton rug is from the Flitterman Collection.

Above • A painting by Morris Louis presides over the living room. Two smaller works are by Janna Syvänoja. The cabinet is nineteenth-century Baltic. A sofa and club chairs by Jonas and gilt armchairs by Michael S. Smith surround a vellum coffee table by Mattaliano. The desk is Louis XVI. The library can be seen beyond the doorway to the left.

Top right • An Ed Moses painting hangs over a banquette covered in a Fortuny cotton.

Bottom right • The work on paper is by Cy Twombly. The Michael S. Smith gilt armchair is upholstered in a custom-woven ombré fabric.

This page • In the kitchen, which opens to a cutting garden, the cabinetry was designed by Ferguson & Shamamian and the hardware is by Nanz.

Opposite • The east-facing morning terrace takes advantage of sunrise views. The furniture is from Sutherland.

Top left • The parchment wallpaper in the master bedroom is by Michael S. Smith for his Jasper Collection. An antique Russian commode serves as a night table.

Above left • A son's bathroom features a shelving unit by British designer Peter Marigold and a sconce by Roman Thomas.

Above right • A walnut desk in a corner of the sitting room is by Thomas Hayes. The Swallowtail armchair is by designer Brian Fireman.

The chandelier in the sitting room is a Branching Bubble by Lindsey Adelman. Above the sofa hangs an Edo-period Japanese screen called *Four Woods*. The standing lamp is by Chris Lehrecke. A carved-walnut side table is by Stefan Bishop, and the coffee table is from JF Chen. In the foreground is a Hans Wegner Flag Halyard chair. The ceramics are by Bari Ziperstein.

Above • Antique urns on the loggia are from Lee Stanton Antiques. The mirror is by Michael S. Smith.

Right • The rattan furniture on the south-facing loggia is by Soane Britain. Like the mirrors, the consoles are by Michael S. Smith.

Above, right, and overleaf • At the back of the house, a flight of steps leads down to the pool, which enjoys a panoramic view toward the Getty Center. The outdoor furniture is from Mecox Gardens.

GARCIA HOUSE

WHEN JOHN MCILWEE, FINANCIAL ADVISOR
to more than a few Hollywood stars, first visited John Lautner's
iconic Garcia House, he and his husband, Bill Damaschke, had
no intention of moving, which just goes to show how easily a
mid-century modern masterpiece perched on the edge of a sun-
soaked cliff can seduce even the most analytical person. "I'm
usually the voice of reason," McIlwee says. "The house needed
work, and it was so inconveniently far up in the Hills, but I'm a
tremendous believer in kismet—and it spoke to us."

Built in 1962, the Garcia House's hallmarks—upswept roofs,
sinuous and geometric shapes, and bold use of steel, glass, and
neon colors—remained intact, but some elements had been
executed with materials that didn't hold up over the years. Before renovating, the couple decided to live in the house for
a year, giving them time to restock the coffers and study Lautner's original drawings, which, thankfully, were in the
Getty archives. "It was a necessary exercise, enabling us to make design choices suited to twenty-first-century living.
We extended the swoop of the roof out twelve feet to protect the glass from the sun because the living room baked. We
never would have known this."

For guidance, the couple hired a team whose pedigrees and credentials were as impressive as the house itself. For
the architectural remodeling, the couple called upon Marmol Radziner, the firm behind the restoration of Richard
Neutra's 1946 Kaufmann House. The roof was replaced, layer upon layer of paint was stripped, black Formica in the
master bath was replaced with honey onyx and glass tiles, and a sliding glass door was added between the living room
and the television room to create a more organic flow.

Interior designer Darren Brown, a former director of Jonathan Adler's interior design studio, introduced glamorous
touches, most notably pieces by Lucite furniture designer Charles Hollis Jones, including a four-poster bed in the master bedroom and a coffee table that was first designed for a Learjet. "He went crazy, in a good way," says McIlwee. The
couple supplemented these furnishings with more earthbound pieces by mid-century designers Vladimir Kagan and

Opposite • Built in 1962, John Lautner's iconic Garcia House displays
the mid-century master's hallmarks: upswept roofs, sinuous curves,
geometric shapes, and bold use of steel, glass, and neon colors.

Above • A vintage Lucite table in the media room was designed
by Charles Hollis Jones.

Paul Evans. "We tried to find pieces that were architecturally inclined," adds McIlwee.

Tweaking and perfecting every surface can hardly be pulled off overnight, and renovations can test the limits of human patience, but the couple rarely wavered. To oversee the finishing touches, McIlwee camped out in a sleeping bag.

"Vincent Gallo, who owned the house before us, said it would change our lives, and it really did, but in unexpected ways," says McIlwee. "Working on this house together threw us into a different realm." McIlwee went from knowing next to nothing about Lautner to becoming a member of the John Lautner Foundation board, and the door to the house remains open to architecture students and museum tours. "Explaining a Lautner house to someone who has never seen one can be ungratifying; it's an immersive experience." Even changing a light bulb has taken the couple into challenging new territory because the house's ceilings are so high and curved. Luke Wood, who owns the John Lautner house Silvertop, said, "We become caretakers, stewards for these properties."

Top • A view through the house looks out over Nichols Canyon toward the ocean and Santa Catalina Island beyond.

Center • The upper hallway is referred to as the "upper deck."

Above • At the base of the stairway leading to the upper hallway, a seating area is adorned with a vintage brass sculpture from Studio 111.

Opposite • From the living area, steps lead up to the dining area. A fiddle-leaf fig with twisted trunk marks the transition.

Overleaf • A Lucite coffee table designed by Charles Hollis Jones for a Learjet centers the living room. A sculpted-metal side table is by Silas Seandel, and the barrel-back club chair is by Milo Baughman. The painting on top of the shelves to the left is by Lisa Yuskavage. Originally, the glass wall featured red, green blue, yellow, and purples panes; only the red, green, and purple remain.

Opposite top • A 1970s Arco floor lamp arches over the living room.

Opposite bottom • The fireplace surround is made from honed granite. The glass table lamp is by Venini.

Above • Master architectural photographer Julius Shulman shot the house in 1972.

Opposite and above • In the dining/kitchen area, vintage Karl Springer chairs surround a Warren Platner table with a smoked-glass top.

Opposite top • Photographs by Cindy Sherman and Gregory Crewdson and a painting by Jan-Ole Schiemann line a wall in the master bedroom. The sofa is from Rago Arts and Auctions.

Opposite bottom • A work by Soo Kim hangs over the Lucite four-poster bed by Charles Hollis Jones. The octagonal bedside table was found in a Paris flea market.

Above • In a sun-drenched seating area, a vintage Lucite chair is covered with a Donghia fabric. The vintage coffee table and hanging wall cabinet are by Paul Evans. The painting, *Interior with Chandelier (after Tarkovsky)*, 2008, is by Kirsten Everberg, and the pottery is from Germany.

Above and opposite • John McIlwee and Bill Damaschke asked Marmol Radziner, the architect who restored the house for them, to add a pool. He based it on John Lautner's original plans.

INDEPENDENT THINKING

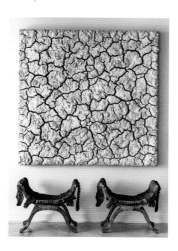

FIROOZ ZAHEDI AND BETH RUDIN DeWoody's vertical compound in a mid-century modern apartment house in Westwood perfectly reflects their shared vision of collecting: a deep and abiding passion for art based on pleasure rather than profit. "I never purchase art as a monetary investment; it's always an emotional investment. It must make me happy and be something I want to look at every day and enjoy," says Zahedi, an Iranian-born photographer who launched his career shooting for Andy Warhol's *Interview* magazine and has contributed to *Vanity Fair* and *Architectural Digest*. His solo show *Elizabeth Taylor in Iran, 1976*, at the Los Angeles County Museum featured the photographs he took of the actress when he accompanied her to Iran on the one trip she took to the country. They remained close friends for the rest of her life.

DeWoody, whose collection of more than 10,000 drawings, paintings, sculptures, photographs, and conceptual works by both iconic and emerging artists is divided among the couple's residences in L.A., New York, and West Palm Beach, has followed the same mantra since she began collecting Beatles paraphernalia at age twelve. "I select art by instinct. I purchase what I like and relate to," she says.

In L.A., Zahedi and DeWoody's bold and deeply personal collections are spread among three apartments in a building designed by architect Victor Gruen that first captured Zahedi's imagination when he was living a block away. "I did a shoot with Billy Wilder there in 1989," the photographer recalls. "The lobby was so grand. I thought, Wow, this would be a very nice place to live."

"My apartment," Zahedi says, "serves as a home, a guest apartment, a mini studio, an office, and a gallery to display my own work. It is different from the other two apartments because the furniture and art are from my collecting over the years here in L.A., including silkscreens that were a gift from Andy Warhol when I worked at *Interview* back in the '70s." Gray walls and thick Persian rugs also read more masculine than the couple's shared spaces.

Opposite • In the foyer of Firooz Zahedi and Beth Rudin DeWoody's apartment in a 1958 building designed by Austrian-born architect Victor Gruen, visitors are greeted by Andrew Brischler's *Vertigo*, an Anne Collier photograph, a Lalanne sheep, and a bear-head sculpture by Otani Workshop. The tables are from John Dickinson.

Above • A work by Bosco Sodi hangs above two Lalanne benches.

Artfully composed on a wall in the living room is a selection of works by California artists, including Ed Ruscha, John Baldessari, Richard Pettibone, Billy Al Bengston, Jonas Wood, and Chuck Arnoldi.

While renovating the apartment that they had designated as their main living space, the couple learned that a double-size unit had just come on the market. DeWoody immediately ran upstairs to check it out and decided that it was better suited to be their primary residence. They turned over the architectural planning of the space they had been working on to Stephen Tomar and Stuart Lampert, and it became their guest apartment. With the help of contractor Greg Greenwood, they then set about tailoring the larger, brighter space to accommodate their collections.

Walls were taken down to create an airy, light-filled living room, divided into two seating areas by a screen-like sculptural installation by artist Joel Otterson. Bleached-wood floors, white walls, and mid-century furniture covered in neutral-colored fabrics allow the art to take center stage. Some pieces were relocated from the couple's New York and Florida houses; others were found through dealers in Dallas and Palm Springs. Zahedi's friend Jim Goodrich of Cache Antiques on Melrose Avenue reupholstered furniture, built beds, found rugs, and fine-tuned everything. Together, Zahedi and DeWoody curated and hung the art. The unstudied mix, as much about accretion as style, results in a level of sophistication that makes traditional elegance seem almost trite by comparison.

Filled with vintage ceramics from DeWoody's collection, a screen by artist *Joel Otterson* divides the living room, beyond which can be seen a vintage Harvey Probber couch. Rooz perches on one of two mid-century sofas that curve around a vintage Philip and Kelvin LaVerne coffee table, along with a two-sided thrift-store sofa flanked by two Lalanne monkey-base tables. To the right, a work by Channa Horwitz hangs over an Adrian Pearsall sofa. On the cocktail table in front of the sofa is a cast-resin sculpture by DeWain Valentine. To the left are works by Matthew Barney and Carol Bove.

Alex Katz's portrait of DeWoody's mother dominates the study,
which also includes works by Robert Hudson, Victor Vasarely, Rachel
Owens, Claudio Verna, Josh Bailer Losh, and Robert Arneson.
The mid-century modern mosaic-topped table was purchased in
Palm Springs.

Top • In the dining room, works by Enrico Cavalli, Peter Alexander, and Sydney Butchkes surround a mid-century modern dining table and chairs. A sculpture by Jeff Colson serves as a centerpiece.

Above • The bar is adorned with sculptures by Alexander Noll and trompe l'oeil book paintings by Martin McMurray.

Above • A Dennis Ekstrom painting hangs over sculptures from Yassi Mazandi's *Flower Series* and a small floral sculpture by Matt Wedel.

Opposite top left • A photo by Firooz Zahedi hangs next to a work by Ed Ruscha.

Opposite top right • Works by Ed Moses and Sister Mary Corita hang over a mid-century modern table topped by a Claire Falkenstein sculpture.

Opposite bottom • Two Ed Moses works hang above a sofa found in Palm Beach. A sculpture by Saloua Raouda Choucair stands to the left.

Opposite • A mid-century room divider, salvaged during the renovation, was repurposed as a headboard in the master bedroom. The large ceramic vase is by Brian Rochefort; the porcelain vase on the bedside table is by Rosenthal. The work hanging to the left of the bed is by Claudio Verna. The work in the hall leading to the bedroom is by Tom Wesselmann.

Above • A guest room features a large painting by Zak Ové. Vincent Szarek's *Rio Arriba*, 2015, hangs over the bed. The lamp and bedside table are from Design Utopia. On the table are a Brian Rochefort ceramic vessel and a Claes Oldenburg *Calico Bunny Blue*.

Overleaf top left • The exuberant, art-filled guest apartment includes works by Ron Davis (top) and Eben Goff.

Overleaf bottom left • Works by (from top to bottom) Noah Purifoy, Pedro Friedeberg, and Jason McLean.

Overleaf right • The art fairly pops against the white walls and floor of the guest apartment living room. Works by James Lee Byars hang on the far wall. To the left, a David Wojnarowicz painting hangs above a Piero Fornasetti table and a Pedro Friedeberg Hand Chair. The ceramic faces on the coffee table are by Joakim Ojanen. The two sofas are by Warren Platner.

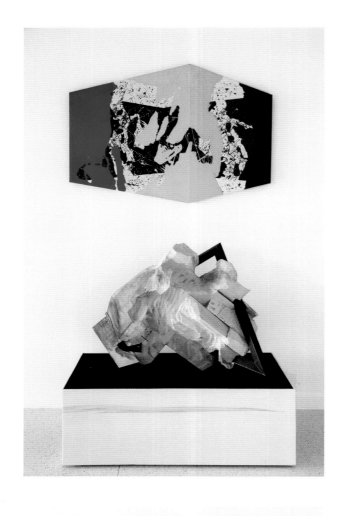

I'VE BEEN RICH AND I'VE BEEN POOR. BELIEVE ME, RICH IS BETTER.

Opposite, clockwise from top left • A Frank Stella lithograph hangs above Yassi Mazandi *Flower* sculptures and Rosenthal vases in Firooz Zahedi's office; a work by Firooz Zahedi; an Andy Warhol *Marilyn Monroe* silkscreen over a Leroy Lamis Lucite sculpture and small Lucite pieces by Vasa Mihich; a Firooz Zahedi photograph of Diane Keaton above a photograph by Adolph de Meyer.

Right • *Neil Armstrong* by Des Lawrence hangs at the end of a hallway lined with works by Firooz Zahedi, Herb Ritts, Rob Wynne, and Dennis Hopper.

Above • Two mid-century modern chairs In Zahedi's office are by Maurice Bailey. The vintage candelabra are from the Beverly Hills Hilton. On the shelves are vintage hat molds and a Vasarely vase.

Overleaf • The art in Zahedi's office includes his photo of Andy Warhol, a Warhol *Mick Jagger* silkscreen, vintage prints by Philippe Halsman, a collage by Zahedi, paintings by Gene Davis, a series of Zahedi photos from an exhibition, a charcoal drawing by Joel Shapiro, and a painting by Ed Moses. A barrel-back club chair is by Milo Baughman, and the side tables in the foreground are by Paul Frankl.

Left • A vintage toy train set sits on the windowsill in the kitchen.

Below • Zahedi kept the original 1958 kitchen cabinetry intact, adding a linoleum floor, Caesarstone counters, and stainless-steel appliances.

Opposite top • A Milo Baughman chair sits under a work by Zahedi in the bedroom of his apartment.

Opposite bottom • A work by Edward Kienholz hangs over the bed. Vintage Fornasetti lamps sit atop mid-century thrift-store cabinets. The bedspread is vintage Moroccan.

CLASSICISM IN HANCOCK PARK

WHEN NEW ORLEANS NATIVE SUZANNE Rheinstein arrived in Los Angeles in the 1970s, she brought along a predilection for easy elegance, a wide-ranging knowledge of period objects, and a keen interest in interior design. "I grew up in a well-appointed, comfortable home, and as a literature major in college, I was just as interested in what Proust's house looked like as I was in his writing."

Since the birth of her now-adult daughter, Kate, Rheinstein and her late husband, Fred, lived in a perfectly proportioned Georgian Revival house in the historic Windsor Square section of Hancock Park. She furnished it early on with a carefully edited selection of family antiques, including the stripped-pine mantelpiece and the two panels of nineteenth-century painted wallpaper in the living room.

Determined to lend the traditional room a breezy feeling more congruent with her adopted state, rather than resort to the glazed chintzes and saturated colors of her childhood, Rheinstein selected hand-blocked linens, which she used on the reverse side, instantly achieving a sun-faded patina. She stippled and glazed the walls in tranquil blue-gray and covered the floor in straw matting. The dining room was painted in translucent stripes of glazing liquid, which glinted in the California sun, creating an interior that was not only correct and elegant but also completely unpretentious and casual.

Parties at the Rheinsteins' were as refined and relaxed as the skilled hostess herself. Jazz pianist Geoff Aymar would play on an old Chickering piano from her husband's childhood home. Doors would be flung open and guests would spill out onto the terrace and around the pool beyond. In the evenings, seemingly hundreds of votive candles would illuminate the haute entertaining and networking. Rheinstein's wide circle of friends proved an unlikely business asset; everyone wanted to be invited to her home, and eventually, they called upon her to design their own homes. Suzanne Rheinstein's name became synonymous with a new L.A. design aesthetic, the defining qualities of

Opposite • In the living room of Suzanne Rheinstein's neo-Georgian house, an eighteenth-century French painted bergère sits in front of a nineteenth-century English demilune table. The lacquer tray holds a pre-Columbian figure, an early Chinese jar, and a Japanese Shibayama piece—a boar's tusk inlaid with mother-of-pearl insects. The portrait of her daughter, Kate, is by Isabel Wadsworth.

Above • An English neoclassical vase, an Etruscan terra-cotta foot fragment, and a late eighteenth-century pen-and-ink wash drawing of a funerary monument surrounding a silhouette are displayed on a Charles X table.

which are often described as elegant civility encompassing a mixture of beautiful objects, furniture styles, art, painted surfaces, and attention to comfort, textures, details, and light. "I use many classic pieces but in a spare way, with lots of room to breathe," she says.

Some thirty years after she moved in, the Windsor Square house remains a prime example of her work and, as is the case with most of Rheinstein's interiors, has stood the test of time. Indeed, its graciousness has only been enhanced by a steady addition of personal mementos collected on the Rheinsteins' world travels. She favors eighteenth-century handicrafts made by women to amuse themselves, including *coquillage* (shell-work), *cartonnage* (cardboard crafting), and *dessins habillés* (fashion drawings).

Her first client, for whom she has decorated three houses and counting, is still her best friend. They continue to go on collecting trips around the world together. Because first and foremost, Rheinstein is a lover of people and parties. As playful as she is resolute, Rheinstein is both den mother and doyenne of the L.A. design world. Her most loyal student is her daughter, Kate, who has followed in her mother's footsteps and runs an interior design business in New York.

Opposite • Richard Buckner's nineteenth-century portrait of English expats in Italy hangs in the entrance hall. Glazed-linen walls in the color of café au lait are trimmed in red grosgrain and accented with Georgian Revival overdoors. A 1929 Chickering piano is from Rheinstein's late husband's family.

Below • Rheinstein's perfectly proportioned Georgian Revival house sits in the historic Windsor Square section of Hancock Park. The groundcover is star jasmine punctuated with boxwood balls, cones, and hedges. White Lady Banks roses climb up the house's façade.

Overleaf • In the living room, an early nineteenth-century tea table with an entwined dolphin pedestal is flanked by chairs covered in Rheinstein's Garden Roses fabric for Lee Jofa, used on the reverse side to create a watercolor, hand-blocked effect. The panels of antique wallpaper are from the New York City townhouse where her late husband was raised.

Left • Portraits of an English farmer's prize cattle hang in the kitchen. Rheinstein designed the farm table.

Below • The house boasts a book-filled garden room that also serves as a spot for intimate suppers. Eighteenth-century portraits of Venetian doges stand out against the yellow-green walls.

Opposite • Next to the garden room, a morning room looks out to the garden. 1920s English Regency-style chairs surround an eighteenth-century English table.

Above • In the dining room, a Baltic chandelier illuminates watercolors by the Lewis family, who were famed ornithological painters.

Opposite • An eighteenth-century portrait, purchased in Venice, graces the stairway. Painted wooden fringe adds a lighthearted touch to Georgian-style curtains. The lantern was found in a Connecticut antiques market.

Left • Rheinstein and a carpenter hand-painted the walls of the master bath in 1983.

Opposite top left and above • The windows in the master bedroom are draped in a fabric Rheinstein designed for Lee Jofa. The bed is antique French, and the floor is painted in a pattern inspired by the floor of Sybil Connolly's living room in Dublin.

Above and opposite top left and right • Rheinstein's inviting bedrooms typically include decoratively painted floors or walls, lavish custom bedding, and personal art to add ambience. Both the curtain fabric in this bedroom and the wallpaper of the en suite bathroom are in Mrs. Geraldine Monro's iconic Lily & Auricula pattern.

Opposite bottom • In another guest room, designed with Rheinstein's granddaughters in mind, the walls are painted to suggest a whimsical tent. The beds are from Anthropologie.

Top left • Rheinstein designed a chaise with a delightful scalloped awning, inspired by summers on the Côte d'Azur.

Top right • Over an outdoor sofa hangs a mock trophy of arms consisting of old garden implements assembled on an antique panel found in England. The paving is bluestone.

Above • A tall hedge screens the pool from the rest of the property, creating a sense of privacy and escape.

Opposite • The courtyard garden, designed by Judy Horton, features boxwood, myrtle, and privet hedges.

Overleaf • In the pool house, a Civil War–era refectory table from Tennessee is topped with vintage bottles found in a Belgian flea market. They are filled with dried *Allium schubertii* from Rheinstein's garden.

SEASIDE CLARITY

A NARROW STRIP OF SANTA MONICA beachfront has long been considered one of Los Angeles's most exclusive and storied settings. During Prohibition, bootleggers in high-powered boats reportedly made regular liquor deliveries to summer cottages along what was considered "California's Gold Coast," also dubbed the "American Riviera" and "Rolls Royce Row." This low-lying stretch of oceanfront boasted some thirty eclectically styled summer homes whose international fame at the time had less to do with their inventive architecture than with their residents, who included many of Hollywood's bold-faced names. Though the district still boasts its share of celebrity residents, it's now more renowned for a rare assemblage of houses by California's master architects, including Richard Neutra, Wallace Neff, Julia Morgan, John Byers, Paul Williams, and Webber and Spaulding.

The front door of one of these residences, a few feet from the Pacific Coast Highway, opens to reveal a historic house designed in 1938 by Richard Neutra. Its singularity is first announced by a serene courtyard signaling a sense of arrival.

The owner, a third-generation Angeleno, immediately appreciated the setting on a wide swath of beach. It defied the stereotype of waterfront houses on stilts, the ocean crashing underneath. As a lifelong art and architecture devotee, the owner was taken by its mid-century modern design. "My grandfather had hired Richard Neutra to build a house for him, so I knew all about him," she says. "We snapped it up. It wasn't in perfect shape, but fortunately, in the 1980s someone bothered and hired Charles Gwathmey to update the electrical system." Four years later, when the lot next door became available, she and her husband decided to upgrade the original house and incorporate an addition.

They turned to architect Steven Ehrlich to unlock the potential and provide more space that would capture the view without sacrificing privacy or going too big. A wish list included protected outdoor space for their young son, a pool, and a guest apartment. Rather than adding to the original structure, Ehrlich hit upon the elegant solution of building a nearby, light-filled box, the shape of which would take its cues from Neutra's curved windows, and connecting it to the original

Opposite • The addition to a 1938 Richard Neutra house that architect Stephen Erlich designed is a light-filled box connected to the original house by a glassed-in walkway. The mid-century French settee in the foreground is by Guillerme et Chambron and was found at a Paris flea market. The Lucite coffee table is by Charles Hollis Jones and the aluminum-framed armchair is by Warren McArthur.

Above • The staircase is Neutra's original design, but the banister has been updated.

structure by means of a narrow, glassed-in walkway, creating two courtyards. The courtyard to the rear of the addition is a quiet green space with a "living wall" designed by landscape designer Barry Beer; the one in front includes a beachside pool. "The addition complements but doesn't imitate Neutra's original design," says the owner.

The new building has a smooth, poured-concrete floor that suits bare feet when one walks to and from the beach through disappearing pocket doorways that often remain open, creating a plein-air quality. "So much of the beauty of L.A. is using outdoor living space privately. It isn't a huge yard, but psychologically we gain lot of space because the glass makes the interiors and yard feel much bigger."

Inside, materials, furnishings, and details are in keeping with the architecture. Mid-century modern pieces mix with contemporary art; a recent acquisition is an abstract by an eighty-three-year-old Colombian woman, Carmen Herrera. "Mid-century furniture is smaller in scale and suits this house," says the owner. "In the 1930s, people weren't interested in building mega-mansions." The resulting home is self-assured without being grand; Neutra surely would have approved.

Opposite • The owner of the house had admired living walls on her travels to Paris and called upon Mia Lehrer to help her implement a design loosely based on a Sonia Delauney painting. Succulents were planted in a stainless-steel structure equipped with a drip system. The living wall overlooks the courtyard created by Stephen Ehrlich's addition.

Left • In the addition, 1940s bar stools by Warren McArthur are upholstered in pleather.

Overleaf • From the inner courtyard, one can see both the original 1938 Neutra house, on the right, and Ehrlich's addition, both rendered in poured concrete for a coherent look. The owner's standard poodle Choichoi enjoys the cross breeze created when all the pocket doors are open.

Above and opposite bottom • In the living room of the original house, which Neutra called a "winter garden," the curved sofa is by Vladimir Kagan. The other sofas and chairs are by Gio Ponti and were originally in the Hotel Principe in Naples, Italy. 1940s Warren McArthur tables, topped by rare green glass called Vitrolite, were originally designed for a Florida house. The painting is by Jason Martin, and the large turquoise vessels are American Blenko glass.

Opposite top • The seating area on the right features Marco Zanuso chairs and a Jean Prouvé table.

Above and opposite • In the dining room, a T. H. Robsjohn-Gibbings table and Warren McArthur chairs all date from the 1940s. A work by graffiti artist Gajin Fujita hangs over the Biedermeier console, on which are grouped nineteenth- and twentieth-century bronzes, a Robert Graham torso, and a work by KAWS.

Opposite • A mid-century modern Venetian chest adds a strong geometric element to the living room.

Right • Another view of the Jean Prouvé table surrounded by Marco Zanuso seating. The painting on the far right is by Eric Orr.

Below • Two collages by Tony Berlant hang in the living room.

Opposite and above • The pool and gardens were designed by
Barry Beer. The barrel-shaped stainless-steel roof of the new addition
reflects the curves of Neutra's original design.

Overleaf • A sliding wall opens onto the broad Santa Monica beach.

ELEMENTS OF STYLE

WHEN PAMELA SHAMSHIRI PURCHASED a badly bowdlerized house by her design hero, Viennese modernist Rudolph Schindler, she was daunted but undeterred. She knew that a proper renovation would demand time and money that she didn't necessarily have, but she did possess the indefatigable ambition of people who pursue their passion for a living. Shamshiri, designer of the Ace Hotels in Palm Springs and L.A., as well as boutiques for Irene Neuwirth and Opening Ceremony, realized that dismissing the opportunity to contribute to a narrative originated by a twentieth-century design maverick would be akin to a scholar of German literature refusing to study Kafka. "This house really meant something in design history," she says.

Built in 1947 for client Richard Lechner and perched high above Laurel Canyon in the Hollywood Hills, the house's concept was a response to Schindler's fascination with the cliffside adobes of the Pueblo Indians. Walls of glass that let in natural light and give way to leafy views, combined with humble plywood interiors, create the impression of a treehouse, a perfect starting point for Shamshiri, the mother of two sons.

From the beginning, she was mindful not to attempt a pure restoration of Schindler's original work, but rather to preserve the master's hallmarks of economy, elegance, and warmth while injecting the place with twenty-first-century sensibilities. Sheetrock was removed, exposing the original Douglas fir ceiling. Metal window frames were replaced with unadorned versions, a galley kitchen was joined with the den, creating a lofty space that proved more amenable to entertaining immediate and extended family, including her brother and business partner, Ramin, who lives nearby with his family.

In the living room, a stainless-steel surround was returned to the fireplace. Built-in sofas, a pullout dining table, and Schindler's decorative trellis on the ceiling were re-created. A deep cedar soaking tub was installed in the master bathroom; the modern-day addition's extraordinary craftsmanship rendered from humble materials is in keeping

Opposite • In an area of the living room in Pamela Shamshiri's renovated Rudolph Schindler house, a red chair by Michael Boyd stands out against the humble plywood walls. The work above the chair is by John Kapel, a Northern California furniture maker. The small wooden table is by Alma Allen.

Above • A work entitled *NOW* by Shamshiri's friend Doug Aitken glints at the base of the staircase.

Opposite and left • A stainless-steel fireplace surround dominates the living room. The coffee table is a restored Schindler design, as is the trellis decorating the ceiling.

Overleaf • This view of the living room reveals the dining room through a screen of wood columns. The floors are a combination of simple stained construction-grade plywood and Douglas fir. The leather poufs are by Dosa, and the cowhide rugs are by Pure and Grand Splendid.

with Schindler's design philosophy. Thanks to plans and black-and-white photos of the original house, found in the University of California Santa Barbara archives, Shamshiri was able to replicate personal touches, including a bar cart that the architect had built for the Lechners.

The result, Shamshiri likes to think, is something Schindler might have built if he were working today. "I would often say to myself, 'What would Schindler do if he were alive?'" Apparently he would have built a house that, while being an engineering hat trick, feels at one with nature and is as sophisticated as it is simple, where a family can seamlessly circulate between inside and out, as the setting sun casts flickering shadows.

Left • Schindler designed a table that pulls out from the wall. The chairs, also designed by Schindler, are reproductions, as the originals are in the Los Angeles County Museum of Art.

Below left • The Buddha is from Thailand.

Below right • Los Angeles designer John Williams created this child gate.

Opposite • In the dining area of the kitchen, Jean Prouvé's Standard chairs from Vitra surround a table designed by Schindler. The stool is by Alma Allen and the vintage Poul Henningsen light fixture is from Galerie Half.

Left, below, and opposite · The dining room opens onto a terrace that overlooks the pool. The table and chairs are by Dutch designer Piet Hein Eek. A custom cowskin-textured rug is by Commune for Decorative Carpets.

Above and right · Vintage furniture, including an Eames Lounge Chair and Ottoman, and drawings decorate the den. The coffee table is by Alma Allen.

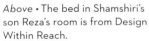

Above • The bed in Shamshiri's son Reza's room is from Design Within Reach.

Top and bottom right • Her son Basel, an avid drum player, chose a neon yellow, Farrow & Ball's Yellow Cake, for his bedroom.

Opposite top left and right • Shamshiri installed a deep cedar soaking tub in the master bathroom.

Opposite bottom • The bed in the master bedroom is by Alma Allen. Shamshiri added the windows and reconfigured the room.

Overleaf • Built in 1947 high in the Hollywood Hills, the house reflects Schindler's fascination with the cliffside adobes of the Pueblo Indians. Matthew Brown and The Tropics designed the garden. Shamshiri repaints the pool a couple of times a year and then allows her children and their friends to "tag" it.

Opposite • A dramatic overhang was part of Schindler's original design.

Right and below • An outdoor dining and barbecue area is off the interior dining room. The large table is in the style of Donald Judd. The deck is made of Douglas fir.

MODERNISM
REDEFINED

IF A DESIGNER'S OWN HOUSE REVEALS
the purest version of their design ethos, then in purchasing a
1990s modernist pavilion, Michael S. Smith flipped the script
on his trademark airy interpretation of English style, divulg-
ing the true breadth of his oeuvre.

In addition to decorating homes for such A-list clients as
George Clooney, Steven Spielberg, Brian Grazer, producer
Laurence Mark, and perhaps most famously, President and
Mrs. Obama, for whom he redecorated the Oval Office and private quarters of 1600 Pennsylvania Avenue, and who remain
loyal clients, Smith also designs furniture, fixtures, fabrics,
and fragrances and has penned four books. He evidently never
wearies of creating and pushing boundaries, so after selling his 1950s slate-roofed Bel Air ranch house lock, stock, and
barrel, Smith embraced the challenges that the modernist pavilion presented.

"It's not the kind of house anyone would really think of building now. You see a lot of houses like this in Spain
and Latin America, built with large volumes for people with large-scale art," says Smith, whose longtime partner,
former television executive James Costos, served as ambassador to Spain and Andorra from 2013 to 2017. Naturally,
during their tenure in Spain, Smith transformed the residence and, by all accounts, elevated entertaining standards.
Informed by his life abroad, Smith put his unusual sensibility—and his talent for uniting wholly disparate objects—
to work.

First he chose to keep the structural intervention subtle, intuitively embracing the original floor-to-ceiling windows,
a seemingly endless polished-limestone floor, and that 1970s punch line, a built-in bar, "I was going to take it out, but
people love it. Everyone gathers there," says Smith.

By joining pieces of different eras and cultures into a single, logical network, Smith created a revelatory, richly tex-
tured modernism that looks to the future. Clean, armless, and affordable sofas from CB2 mix with nineteenth-century

Opposite • In a corner of designer Michael S. Smith's 1990s
modernist pavilion is one of a pair of Steve Chase X Base tables, and
Karl Springer benches. Robert Polidori's photographs *Death of Marat*
and *Salle de Bain, Marie Antoinette* hang near a Claude Lalanne
Miroir Structure Végétale.

Above • Joan Mitchell's *Looking for a Hell*, 1959, hangs over a pair of
Treviso hand-carved gilded armchairs upholstered in Palma Caramel
leather, designed by Smith for his Jasper Collection.

gilded chairs. The art includes an oversized Claude Lalanne mirror, a massive painting by contemporary artist Gary Simmons, and an eighteenth-century "Rubenesque" oil. In the dining room, Karl Springer goatskin-covered chairs surround an early nineteenth-century French mahogany table.

The home's original owner built the 10,000-square-foot one-bedroom house as a party backdrop, which suits Costos and Smith to a T. With residences in Madrid and Palm Springs, and clients around the world, the couple are constantly branching out, connecting and reconnecting, and they delight in bringing the house to life with gatherings at which former presidents and first ladies and European royalty happily mix with guests from the entertainment, art, and design worlds. Everyone circulates seamlessly from the dramatic pavilion to the glamorous courtyard beyond, put at ease by the couple's warmth and hospitality.

Left • An early eighteenth-century George I lacquered and gilded chest with brass mounts sits under an untitled 2008 work by Julian Schnabel.

Below • The south façade features a minimalist sculpture by Tony Smith.

Opposite • An untitled painting by Winfried Virnich simultaneously contrasts and resonates with a pair of George II paw-footed stools.

Overleaf • In the cavernous living room, an allegorical oil painting from the School of Rubens at the far end coexists with Gary Simmons's *Hurricane*, 2013, on the wall over the sofa.

Opposite • In the dining room, an early nineteenth-century Louis-Philippe mahogany table is surrounded by Karl Springer chairs. Two works by Jack Pierson cover one of the walls: *Torse d'Athlete en Marble* and *Burning Palm Fronds*, both 2010.

Above • Beatrice Caracciolo's *Life Lines* and Ludwig Sander's *Adirondack VIII* hang on the other walls in the dining room. A fine Tibetan rug is from Mansour.

Left • In a sitting room, James Nares's *Pizarro's Gold* hangs over the sofa, flanked by a pair of Eve Kaplan's parcel-gilt rocaille mirrors. The vintage three-legged chairs surrounding a Steve Chase X Base table are by Hammond Kroll.

Above • A barrel-back chair by Paul Dupré-Lafon is upholstered in Templeton River Velvet in the Warm Cedar colorway. Philip Taaffe's *Hybrid* adds color to the room.

Above • A Karl Springer stainless-steel bench sits at the foot of a Templeton polished-nickel four-poster bed. The eighteenth-century Japanese screen is from H. M. Luther.

Opposite top • The Levantina marble in the master bathroom is original to the house.

Right • Hanging over a neoclassical gilt-wood console in the entryway to the master bedroom is a print of Wayne Gonzales's *White House*. It holds special meaning for Smith, as he decorated the Oval Office and the private quarters of the Obama White House.

Above and opposite top and bottom • The focal point of the exterior courtyard is a lily pond. The outdoor furniture is a combination of pieces: the wood-topped tables and benches are from CB2's Chelsea outdoor line; the round table and chairs are from the Walter Lamb Collection, and the cushioned sofa and ottoman are from Kreiss.

GEORGIAN REDUX

EVEN AT A YOUNG AGE, RENAISSANCE man Steve Tisch intuitively understood the power of thinking big. As the story goes, during his first visit to Los Angeles in 1964, the teenager tagged along with his parents to a party hosted by actress Polly Bergen and her husband at the time, legendary producer Freddie Fields, at their 1932 Paul Williams–designed Georgian mansion, and from that moment on, he dreamed of a life in L.A. with all the trimmings. Cut to 2010, and Steve Tisch is living in that very house. On display are his Golden Globe and Academy Award for 1994's Best Picture, *Forrest Gump*, and a Vince Lombardi Trophy (for the Giants' victory over the Patriots in 2008; his family owns 50 percent of the team), as well as a world-class art collection.

When it came time to refresh the house, Tisch turned to fellow polymath Peter Dunham, the Oxford-educated and fantastically funny British expat whose seemingly nonchalant interiors are based on encyclopedic design knowledge and astute observations amassed on his world travels. "Steve is the best kind of client—nice person, great house, great taste. He's what we call the Great White Rhino in decorating: a single, rich, straight man. I wish I could clone him."

Dunham's agenda was to create a masculine backdrop for Tisch's contemporary art collection without diminishing the house's Georgian allure. At the same time, he had to make the place comfortable for Tisch's frequent gatherings. "He's not a flashy guy," Dunham says. "He's casual in the way he entertains, and because of his varied interests, he has a broad range of guests, from twenty-five-year-old-barely there filmmakers to his mother's friends, art collectors, and athletes, so it was most important to create a happy and welcoming environment, rather than something intimidating and serious."

To that end, Dunham took a cue from his British upbringing and divided the grand living room into smaller, more intimate seating areas. Upholstery and curtains in stripes and solids, rather than florals and prints, read masculine, as

Opposite and above • Designed in 1932 by architect Paul Revere Williams, Steve Tisch's Georgian-style brick house melds Old World elegance with a fresh, tailored look to accommodate his world-class contemporary art collection. A traditional circular stair hall features prints from Ed Ruscha's book of photographs *Nine Swimming Pools and a Broken Glass.*

Right • A work by Ed Ruscha hangs over an Italian console in the living room.

Far right • A view of the mirrored entry hall from the living room. A plaster chandelier by Waldo's Designs hangs over a 1930s Raymond Subes table. A reproduction of an Ernest Boiceau rug comes from designer Peter Dunham's store, Hollywood at Home. To contrast the formality of the Chinese Chippendale–style niches flanking the doorway into the living room, Dunham suggested a grouping of George Stoll's colorful wax cups.

does furniture with simple, clean lines, including a 1930s Raymond Subes table, chairs by Jean-Charles Moreux, and 1940s Jacques Adnet lamps. Such selections were assured enough to stand up to the important art collection without overpowering it. A colorful collection of wax cups by L.A. artist George Stoll was installed in a pair of Chinese Chippendale–style niches that would usually hold "gems and knickknacks and everything I can't stand," says Dunham.

"When you're in the room, the art isn't fighting for attention. It only becomes fancy if you know what it is. Nothing is pompous," says Dunham. Apple-green French silk curtains in the living room resonate with both a work by Jean-Michel Basquiat and the view out the windows. "Green is very much a neutral in Los Angeles," says Dunham, whose prevailing design philosophy is to blur the lines between indoors and outdoors.

The entrance hall, which leads from the front of the house to the back lawn, with its sweeping view of L.A. beyond, is almost an invisible space. Clad in mirrors, it reflects the gardens but also reminds Tisch of the glamour that attracted him to the house, and indeed, to L.A., in the first place.

Overleaf • Dunham selected a striped fabric to cover vintage armchairs. The abaca rug is by Christopher Farr. A prized Jean-Michel Basquiat painting hangs over a sofa covered in a Claremont linen.

Top left and right • Tisch discreetly displays his awards, including a Vince Lombardi Trophy and an Oscar, in his study.

Above • The armchairs, ca. 1870, are upholstered in a Robert Kime stripe. A painting by Howard Hodgkin hangs over the mantel.

An antique Oushak rug grounds the master bedroom, where curtains and upholstery in neutral-colored fabrics by Claremont create a calm environment. A Diane Arbus photograph hangs to the left of the fireplace; to the right is a work by Hans Hofmann.

Opposite • In a daughter's bedroom, a vintage suzani covers the headboard of a hand-carved canopy bed by Hollywood at Home. The linens are by Deborah Sharpe. The tole chandelier is 1930s French.

Above • A monogrammed headboard graces a custom bed in another daughter's bedroom. The armchair is covered in a John Robshaw fabric.

Overleaf • A seating area in the family rooms opens onto a garden designed by Pamela Burton. Peter Dunham's Fig Leaf linen brightens the room and brings the outdoors in. A vintage Caucasian rug covers an oversize ottoman.

Pages 356 • Armchairs from Hollywood at Home surround a trestle table from Lucca, Italy, in the family room. The custom-made striped kilim comes from Jamal's Rug Collection. A work by John Baldessari hangs over the mantel.

Page 357 • Breakfast and lunch are often enjoyed in a sunny spot off the family room, in the midst of an herb garden.

Above left and right • Sculptures by Thomas Houseago (left) and Ai Weiwei (right) preside over the garden.

Opposite • A Regency-style pool house designed by Appleton & Associates includes guest bedrooms.

VISUAL JOURNEY

THE FAÇADE OF CLIFF AND MANDY

Einstein's house is as unassuming and welcoming as its owners. But a visit to the inner realm of their home is an experience filled with changing narratives, challenging perspectives, and flat-out beauty.

The story begins in 1972, when the Einsteins purchased a former avocado grove and commissioned architect Ron Goldman to create a timeless house in which they would raise their two children. Goldman suggested multilevel, interlocking shapes that incorporated efficiency, economy, and simplicity. Years later, with their children grown, the couple hankered for a new chapter and set about transforming the same house into a strikingly composed universe of contemporary art.

"We wondered what our home would look like if it were transformed into galleries for contemporary art. As we discussed this possibility, we realized that we could really make it happen. And we began what became our great adventure together," says Cliff Einstein. Since then, the couple has collected about 200 works, 120 of which are displayed, with others often on loan to museums. "We wish we could see them all at once."

Their first purchase was John Register's mournful painting of chairs in a sunlit room that seemed to represent older folks who might have gathered there each day. The collection grew to incorporate works by Rufino Tamayo, Sterling Ruby, Kiki Smith, Mark Grotjahn, Matthew Barney, and Mary Weatherford, to name a few.

Over the years, as their passion exceeded their space, the couple imagined replacing a tennis court with a gallery, no small sacrifice for Mandy, who had once been a tennis pro. Again, they turned to Goldman to realize their concept. "He connected the new gallery to our home in a way that was seamless and gave us a dramatic new space and chapter for our collecting," says Cliff. Now the house is a fluid and compelling blend of architecture, art, and landscape. Walls are white, floors are black, and furniture is quiet and classical so as not to distract from the art. Filtered

Opposite • Cliff and Mandy Einstein transformed their house into their own personal art gallery. Displayed in the hallway at the top of the stairs are, clockwise from the sculpture on the ledge: Joana Vasconcelos's Amari, 2012; one of Mai-Thu Perret's Les Guérillères, 2016; Mark di Suvero's Way Through, 1989-90; an untitled 1994 painting by Albert Oehlen; Kishio Suga's Disappeared Space, 2005; and an untitled 1953 painting by John McLaughlin.

Above • Nam June Paik's Bakelite Child, 1986.

Above • In the study, the painting over the armchair is Carroll Dunham's *Small Bather*, 2009–10. On the wall up the stairs is an untitled 1986 work by George Rickey. At right is John Chamberlain's *Cafe Macedonia*, 1984.

Opposite top • The small painting on the wall to the left is Elizabeth Peyton's *Nick Reading Moby Dick*, 2003. On the right is an untitled 2000 photograph by Cindy Sherman.

Opposite bottom • In a hallway, the work on the left is Gilbert and George's *West End*, 2001. To the right is an untitled 1975 work by Sigmar Polke.

natural light in the morning is fresh and uplifting; in the evening, artificial light dramatizes the gallery.

Two of the collection's most significant pieces are located in the garden but are visible from the gallery: Nancy Rubins's gigantic 1997 sculpture made out of airplane parts and *Second Meeting*, a James Turrell skyspace originally created in 1985 for the Museum of Contemporary Art in Los Angeles. The couple planned to commission the artist to make an original piece for their garden when they were told they could have this work. "*Second Meeting* was installed at our home in 1989 and became the first freestanding work from James Turrell." It would eventually spawn nearly a hundred skyspaces throughout the world, each unique. Every year, scaffolding goes up around the Turrell piece so that a crew can restore and sharpen the edges of the square opening in the ceiling. The walls are repainted with a special moisture-resistant paint and the teakwood benches are sanded and oiled like the deck of a ship. "It's probably good that we did not initially realize what maintaining a work like this would entail, but it has become the hallmark of our collection, so we have yet to complain."

Overleaf • In the bar and seating area of the kitchen, Ed Ruscha's *The Long Wait*, 1995, hangs over the bar. Above the fireplace is John Baldessari's *Green Fissure*, 1990. The tiled floor and table in front of the sofa are by Marlo Bartels.

Opposite, clockwise from top left • Rashid Johnson's *Thinking of a Master Plan*, 2012, hangs next to Juan Muñoz's *Standing Arab at London*, 1999; Kerry James Marshall's *Club Couple*, 2014; an untitled 2003 drawing by Mark Grotjahn and, through the doorway on the right, Yayoi Kusama's *Silver Shoes*, 1976; an untitled 1994 painting by Albert Oehlen.

Top • A close-up view of Yayoi Kusama's *Silver Shoes*, 1976.

Above • In the center of the far wall hangs Ed and Nancy Kienholz's *Holdin' the Dog*, 1986. To the right is Sam Gilliam's *Mycenaean Ode*, 1965. The rusted-steel sculpture below it is Tony Cragg's *Administrative Landscape*,1990–91.

Above and opposite • Over a table set with John Gerrard's Bone Cutlery from Artware Editions, hangs Mark Bradford's *Zoom*, 2007.

Overleaf • Visible through the gallery's glass walls are two of the most important works in the Einsteins' collection. To the left is James Turrell's skyspace *Second Meeting*, 1985–86, and to the right is Nancy Rubins's mammoth untitled 1997 sculpture fashioned out of airplane parts.

Opposite and above • *Second Meeting*, installed in 1989, was James Turell's first freestanding work. Annual maintenance includes repainting the walls with moisture-resistant paint and sanding and oiling the teakwood benches.

Overleaf • Nancy Rubins's airplane-parts sculpture appears to teeter precariously over the garden and Thomas Houseago's *Dancer II*, 2010.

CALIFORNIA DREAMING

WHEN ZOË AND OLIVIER DE GIVENCHY moved from London with their growing family in tow, they envisioned living in a house with an authentic sense of place. To Zoë, that meant "a 1920 Paul Williams, which I love, a 1920s Spanish Revival, or a mid-century modern." A house nestled in the foothills of the Santa Monica Mountains with a sweeping view of their adopted city became an obvious choice. "I thought, if we're going to live in L.A., I want to see it," Zoë says.

Designed in 1961 by Harold Levitt, the house is located in storied Trousdale Estates, a Beverly Hills neighborhood that boasts a constellation of houses by Levitt and other mid-century masters, including Wallace Neff, Paul R. Williams, A. Quincy Jones, Frank Lloyd Wright, and Allen Siple.

Levitt's architectural hallmarks—an exaggerated overhang, expanses of glass, exposed-stone walls, a kidney-shaped pool, and other water features—were intact. "Unlike a lot of houses that we saw, this one, despite having been completely renovated, remained true to its roots. In L.A., it's rare to find but worth seeking out," Zoë notes.

After editing the interiors to create a "blank slate," the couple installed a carefully curated and artful mix of pieces from their London home and from the collections of their respective families, "to bring a sense of warmth and familiarity." Billy Baldwin chairs mix with a Boulle-style desk, a sculpture by Robert Courtright, pastel paintings and collages by Olivier's beloved uncle, iconic French couturier Hubert de Givenchy, and Philippe Venet, Olivier's godfather. To create a division between the entrance foyer and the living room without diminishing the flow of space or light, Olivier designed two airy, geometrically patterned screens, which a local artisan rendered in walnut. Upon installation, the couple realized that Olivier's design bore a resemblance to Hubert de Givenchy's logo.

"Life here is such a contrast to London," Zoë says. "Everything opens up completely. There's just endless sunshine." When the sun does set, the house is bathed in neon purple and pink light in the winter, orange and yellow in the summer, and the view is a carpet of city lights.

Opposite • In the library of Zoë and Olivier de Givenchy's house, designed in 1961 by Harold Levitt, is an oil portrait of their daughter by English painter Julia Condon.

Above • A photo of Olivier's uncle, the late Hubert de Givenchy, and Audrey Hepburn.

Above • A dramatic living wall, designed and installed by Patrick Blanc, greets visitors at the entrance.

Opposite top left • Two paintings in the entrance hall are by Chinese artist Huang Rui, one of the founders of the Chinese contemporary art movement.

Opposite top right • The small collage is by Olivier's godfather, Philippe Venet. The screens dividing the foyer and a hallway from the living room were designed by Olivier and rendered in walnut by architectural designer Alexander Deutschman.

Opposite bottom • The bronze sculpture is one of a pair, *Ulysses* and *Penelope*, by Hungarian sculptor Laszlo Taubert. A grouping of small drawings, lithographs, and collages lines the hall leading from the living room to the bedrooms.

Opposite top • In the living room, a pair of Carlo de Carli chairs covered in black velvet flanks a sinuously curving pair of Brazilian rosewood coffee tables. The sofa is by Nicky Kehoe.

Opposite bottom • The painting above the fireplace is by Los Angeles artist Mark Russell Jones. Lazslo Taubert's bronze sculptures *Ulysses* and *Penelope* flank the fireplace.

Above • The airy, light-filled living room overlooks the pool.

The dining room chairs are covered in two shades of velvet by Quadrille. The collage is by Philippe Venet.

Zoë de Givenchy designed the round walnut and powder-coated-steel table. It was made and installed by Alexander Deutschman. The Stalingrad Primo chandelier is from Bourgeois Bohème in Los Angeles.

Above • This brass bed with a grasscloth-covered headboard and canopy was designed by Zoë de Givenchy and built by Alexander Deutschman. The linens are by John Robshaw and Frette. A mid-century waterfall bench is upholstered in Schumacher gold velvet. The oil painting above the bed is by Russian painter Elena Gorokhova. The carpet, bed skirt, and bolsters are by Elizabeth Eakins.

Opposite • In the master bath, the seat of an eighteenth-century prayer chair is covered in a Raoul Textiles fabric. The Victoria + Albert Napoli tub looks out on the lawn and the canyon beyond.

Overleaf • The de Givenchys were attracted to the house in large part because its mid-century architectural hallmarks—exaggerated overhangs, broad expanses of glass, and kidney-shaped pool—were intact. The outdoor furniture is by Danish design firm Norm Architects.

Pages 388–89 • The de Givenchy children play on the west-facing lawn overlooking the Trousdale Estates neighborhood of Beverly Hills.

ACKNOWLEDGMENTS

To all the architects, designers, decorators, and artists
who have made Los Angeles such a special place.

LOS ANGELES REMAINS A CITY BEHIND closed doors, so we are deeply grateful to the homeowners, architects, interior designers, garden designers, and friends who opened their houses, gave freely of their time, and trusted us with the stories of how their residences came to life. There would be no book without the generosity of: Don Bachardy, Tim Campbell, Joel Chen, Zoë and Olivier de Givenchy, Peter Dunham, Cliff and Mandy Einstein, Waldo Fernandez, Cliff Fong, Oliver Furth, Sarah Gavlak, Dierdre and Tony Graham, Mark Haddawy, Poonam Khanna, Margo Leavin, Art Luna, Mickey Madden, John McIlwee and Bill Damaschke, Jane and Marc Nathanson, David and Liz Netto, Susan Nimoy, Ann Philbin and Cynthia Wornham, Suzanne Rheinstein, Richard Shapiro, Mark D. Sikes and Michael Griffin, Pamela Shamshiri, Ramin Shamshiri, Michael S. Smith and James Costos, Darren Star, Madeline Stuart, Steve Tisch, Hope Warschaw, Kelly Wearstler, Ruth and Hutton Wilkinson, and Kulapat Yantrasast.

Jennifer Ash Rudick and Firooz Zahedi

I moved to Los Angeles because I was seduced by Hollywood. In time I came to fall in love not just with the city's climate and terrain but also with its architecture and design. Many talented architects had settled in and around Los Angeles and, seeing all that space and natural beauty, they took the opportunity to experiment with modernist ideas that changed the way people lived. They created homes that enhanced both family and social life with simple yet beautiful lines and layouts—all without losing their artistic integrity or individual style.

City of Angels showcases homes by several of these great talents. I am therefore most grateful to Nina and Mark Magowan for asking me to be the photographer for this project and for giving me the freedom to choose most of the homes. I am also indebted to the rest of the great team at Vendome Press for their hard work in making this book so special. Some people skip reading the text that accompanies a book filled with photographs, but I was delighted to work with our author, Jennifer Ash Rudick, whose thoroughly researched text splendidly balances the photographs in the book.

I am also thankful to my photographic support team: my first assistant, Frank Schaefer, who's a technical "whiz," and my other great assistant, Eric Axene, both of whom are talented photographers themselves. I am indebted to Saeed Babaeean of Empty Vase in West Hollywood for supplying the beautiful flowers that enrich the images in this book. Particular thanks to my son, Darian Zahedi, for taking such a wonderful portrait of me for the book. Last but not least, I thank my wife, Beth Rudin DeWoody, who introduced me to Mark and Nina and who gave me great guidance in choosing some of the homes featured in the book.

Firooz Zahedi

This book owes everything to the expert guidance of everyone at Vendome Press. Mark and Nina Magowan led this project from beginning to end with care and creativity. Their discerning eye, unflappability, and kindness are priceless. I am beyond thankful to polymath Jackie Decter, whose thoroughness, diligence, candor, and friendship made every stage of the book a complete joy. Celia Fuller's unerring taste and striking design brought the photographs and text to life. Thank you to Jim Spivey for keeping production on schedule and Meghan Phillips for her diplomacy and tenacity, ensuring that the book lands on the right desks. Beatrice Vincenzini's continued enthusiasm carries the day.

This book's splendor is indebted to the extraordinary talent and diligence of photographer Firooz Zahedi. How fortunate we are that Firooz agreed to explore and document L.A.'s domestic life with his camera. His deft navigation of narrow, twisting roads is only surpassed by the clarity and precise composition of his work.

I would be completely lost without the influence of my mother, Agnes Ash, who is a brilliant example that there is pleasure in hard work and collaboration and whose own writing reminds me to look for humanity in every story. I am forever grateful to Clarke and Amelia Rudick, who remain unfailingly encouraging of these endeavors. The greatest gratitude goes to Joe Rudick, who is the first to read text, the last to complain about an unpredictable schedule, and the champion behind every project.

Jennifer Ash Rudick

City of Angels: Houses and Gardens of Los Angeles
First published in 2018 by The Vendome Press
Vendome is a registered trademark of The Vendome Press, LLC

NEW YORK
Suite 2043
244 Fifth Avenue
New York, NY 10001
www.vendomepress.com

LONDON
63 Edith Grove
London,
UK, SW10 0LB
www.vendomepress.co.uk

Distributed in North America by Abrams Books
Distributed in the United Kingdom, and the rest of the world,
by Thames & Hudson

ISBN 978-0-86565-357-3

Publishers: Beatrice Vincenzini, Mark Magowan, and Francesco Venturi
Editor: Jacqueline Decter
Production Director: Jim Spivey
Designer: Celia Fuller

Library of Congress Cataloging-in-Publication Data
available upon request

Printed and bound in China by 1010 Printing International Ltd.
First printing

Front endpaper • Los Angeles at dawn, seen from the balcony of
Beth Rudin DeWoody and Firooz Zahedi's apartment, which looks
east over Beverly Hills and the Hollywood Hills toward the iconic
Hollywood sign and the Verdugo Mountains beyond.
Page 1 • In Beth Rudin DeWoody and Firooz Zahedi's apartment,
Jackson DeWoody sits beneath Alex Katz's portrait of his great-
grandmother Gladyce Largever Rudin Begelman (see pages 260–77).
Pages 2–3 • The pool at a splendid neo-Georgian house in Pacific
Palisades enjoys unobstructed views of the Santa Monica Mountains
(see pages 226–45).
Pages 4–5 • Water lilies float in one of three ponds at the home of
art patrons Mandy and Cliff Einstein (see pages 360–75).
Back endpaper • Hollywood in the moonlight, seen from John
Lautner's iconic Garcia House, now owned by John McIlwee and
Bill Damaschke, high in the Hollywood Hills.